Breaking Free from

BOOMERANG LOVE

HEALING
EMPOWERMENT
AND FREEDOM
FROM
ABUSE

Getting Unhooked from
ABUSIVE
BORDERLINE
RELATIONSHIPS

LYNN MELVILLE

Illustrated with Pot-Shots® ('Brilliant Thoughts'®)
by Ashleigh Brilliant

WHAT OTHERS ARE SAYING ABOUT THIS BOOK

As a psychotherapist dealing with borderline personality disordered people for the last 19 years, I'm thrilled to finally see a book written by a partner of BPDs for other partners.

I've served as the online therapist for the Land of Oz Internet community board (LandofOz@yahoo.groups.com) for the past five years. I've seen literally hundreds, if not thousands, of partners post on this site, begging for information and support to help them deal with the pain and confusion of their relationships with BPDs.

I'm pleased to now have *Boomerang Love* to recommend to them. It will be a lifeline to throw to them in their beaten-down despair.

— *Elyce M. Benham, MS, NCC, CCFC, LPC*

Lynn Melville's book, *Boomerang Love* is an excellent resource for someone who is caught in the cycle of violence. While not all abusers have a personality disorder, as Melville points out, the important thing is to focus on yourself, to 're-connect with yourself.' This is the only way out of an abusive relationship, since we cannot change someone else's behavior. Melville's straight-forward approach to focusing on one's self can be very helpful to anyone affected by an abusive partner.

— *Rebecca Robertson, Executive Director,*
Domestic Violence Solutions for Santa Barbara County

Thank you, thank you, *Boomerang Love*! Not knowing that I was really dealing with a personality disorder with my partner, I divorced him. I later forgave his behavior and took him back again … only to see the old painful relationship return, this time worse than before. Reading *Boomerang Love* allowed me to finally see that I could neither heal my partner, nor bear the pain of living with him, and I got out.

— *Barbara Spencer*

When I was going through the ending of my marriage, I was sure my husband was crazy … or maybe it was *I* who was the crazy one. I read *Boomerang Love* 25 years later, and so many of the behaviors I could never understand became clear to me. I wish this book had been available to me and my children at the time of my divorce from their dad. We would have been able to understand that their dad couldn't love my children or father them as they needed, because of his mental disorder. So much hurt and grief would have been avoided. I urge anyone who is dealing with a painful, abusive relationship to read this book. The tragedy is in expecting normal behaviors from someone who is so deeply injured that they cannot function with awareness of the suffering of another.

— *Pat Haley*

❈ I have read five books on BPD and have made the announcement to friends that your book is the sixth and final. I am ending my quest to understand this heinous condition with your book. For me, your book is the best closure. It's time for me to move on after four years of mourning the loss of him and the marriage. Thanks so much for the book. You rock.

❈ I have been pushing your book. It's awesome! I am halfway through and lived every page with you, along with many others. Thanks for sharing with all of us your pain and confusion. If I had to choose one word to describe my life with my BPD, it would be 'confused.' I was constantly confused.

❈ What you said (in *Boomerang Love*) struck a chord with me. No one understands how hurt and upset I am. Yes, I have to walk away. But walking away from something you love is so very hard. You are forced to internalize. Your book has shown me that I can do it! And even more so, I will! Thank you.

❈ It was amazing to read your book. I sat there with a highlight pen, highlighting the statements in your book that I had said to my partner – never knowing that others were saying the same thing! I am love, I give every ounce of myself. I am a magnet for these people – but never will I be again!

❈ Thank you for putting into words exactly what was going on in my relationship. Of all the books I've read on BPD, yours was the most informative. It gave me the strength to move on. (I'm eight months removed from a ten-year nightmare.)

❈ As I read your book, I felt as though I was reading a journal of my chaotic marriage with my borderline wife, except I was reading your words. Your book belongs in the office of every therapist, as it provides a rare insight into the life of a person in the difficult position of recovering from the abuse sustained in a borderline relationship.

❈ Though my relationship was long ago, the devastation left following the storm had left me numb to life for quite a number of years. Reading your book and then knowing that there was an actual 'name to my pain' (borderline personality disorder) was like salve to my wounds, the healing element that had been missing all these years. At last I knew the 'why's.' Going back and re-living my pain, this time with 'new eyes' that understood BPD, released those many years of pent-up pain.

Breaking Free from

BOOMERANG LOVE

Getting Unhooked from

ABUSIVE
BORDERLINE
RELATIONSHIPS

Other books by Lynn Melville:

Reality Checks from Boomerang Love –
Lifelines for People Caught in Abusive
Relationships

ALSO RECOMMENDED:

One Way Ticket to Kansas by Ozzie Tinman

(Another book written by a partner to a Borderline)

Breaking Free from

BOOMERANG LOVE

Getting Unhooked from

ABUSIVE
BORDERLINE
RELATIONSHIPS

by Lynn Melville

Illustrated with Pot-Shots® ('Brilliant Thoughts'®)
by Ashleigh Brilliant

Melville Publications

Breaking Free from Boomerang Love:
Getting Unhooked from Abusive Borderline Relationships
by Lynn Melville

> **Please note that the last name I bear now does not
> belong to the BPD partner I refer to in this book.**

Published by
Melville Publications
PO Box 2036
Santa Maria, CA 93457-2036
Web sites: www.boomeranglove.com
www.stoptheabuse.blogs.com

Ashleigh Brilliant's web site: www.ashleighbrilliant.com

Printed in the United States of America

TABLE OF CONTENTS

The greatest thing a human soul ever does in this world is to see something and to tell what it saw in a plain way. Hundreds of people can talk for one who can think, but thousands can think for one who can see.

— John Ruskin, *Modern Painters*

DEDICATION

In memory of my father, John Croghan, who never knew the *name of his pain* – borderline personality disorder. He bravely struggled on in his marriage to my alcoholic, borderline personality disordered mother so he could love and raise his four children.

He was 79 when my mother died. He had two and a half years of freedom from his cage before he died of a sudden heart attack.

Thanks, Dad ... I miss you.

Acknowledgments

This book is really a book of love and compassion for the reader – from me as the person who experienced the pain and chronicled the journey – but also from all my family and friends who have encouraged me to keep on working to get it published. They have *so* believed in the message of *Boomerang Love* and the need to make it available to those people still struggling in the trenches with narcissistic borderline personality disordered partners.

To my front line of cheerleaders – Gwen Curry, Pat Haley, Kathy Stoddard, Jim Gunn, Andy Casey, Allene Baichtal, Nina Thompson, Karen Miller, Craig and Jennie Hamlin, and JS – thank you for continuing to urge me forward when life intervened to take my attention away from this important book. And thanks to my daughters, Carrie and Stacy, for believing in their Mom.

To the many folks on the Land of Oz site for partners of BPDs, and especially Elyce Benham, the psychotherapist/moderator (LandofOz@yahoogroups.com), thank you for listening to my story and helping me to heal. Your site allowed me a safe place to journal my pain and gave me many messages of wisdom and hope.

And a huge thank you to all the wonderful people who so warmly welcomed me into the many 12-Step meetings I attended. Your honest sharing of your stories helped me to see myself clearly – and the steps I needed to take to regain control of my life.

A separate, big hug to Jim Gunn for literally *pushing* me across the finish line to publication. I absolutely could not have done it without his help.

To my editor/book designer, Tony Stubbs, my deepest thanks for your insightful inspirations and professional production of *Boomerang Love's* cover design, text and illustration layout, and compassionate sensitivity to the dilemma of the partners of BPDs. Your sage advice and guidance were invaluable to me.

And finally, a note of gratitude to my ex-BPD partner. Thank you for the lessons, thank you for the strength I received, and thank you for the soul growth.

PREFACE

Boomerang Love? BPD? This book needs a dictionary! Not really. But a few words of explanation will help.

Boomerang Love describes the on-again, off-again behavior some of us have engaged in with our love relationships. We leave the painful relationship ... then go back to it ... then leave it ... then go back to it ... over ... and over ... and over ....

Our partners say they're sorry for their behavior, we're showered with flowers, they promise it'll never happen again ... or worse, we convince *ourselves* that it won't happen again. We pick up the shattered pieces of our relationship and *try* again.

Boomerang Love — catapulting ourselves out of the relationship and out the door — and then turning around and going back through that same door again. Sometimes we make it out one last time — for good ... and go on to find peace and happiness. Other times we're stuck for a lifetime, our friends and families watching helplessly as our mental and physical health take downward turns.

This book is a lifeline to throw to someone in that stuck Boomerang Love spot.

BPD refers to *borderline personality disorder.* The reader will find it listed and described in the Diagnostic and Statistical Manual 4th Edition (DSM-IV) and also in the section of this book titled *Definitions and Behavior Descriptions.*

In my personal Boomerang Love journey, the defining moment came when I discovered the existence of narcissism and borderline personality disorder. At last I had the answers to the *why's* of my painful relationship with my partner. Thus, in my writing in this book, I refer to my partner (and others like him) as a BPD. Mental health professionals make distinctions between the ten personality disorders, but they do agree that the narcissistic personality disorder seems to be an underlying factor in all of the other personality disorders to some extent. For the sake of simplicity and the delivery of the message in this book, the BPD term fits.

However, don't get hung up on mental health criteria or try to *understand* the disorders too deeply at first. Read the following introduction and then jump into the book.

The object is to re-connect with *yourself* – who *you* are and what you're *feeling* in the relationship you're in. Our *feelings* are what lead us to the *actions* we need to take.

Our *heads* have known all along what we needed to do ….

Lynn Melville

Introduction

I remember the day this book started. It was April, 2000, and I was standing in my kitchen, gazing out the window, once again going over the pieces of the last few years of my life like a jigsaw puzzle, trying to make sense of them. Slowly, the words began to come. I had an awareness, an insight, a light-bulb-in-the-head moment.

Ah-hah! I understood a *piece* of *why* the soul-blistering nightmare I had been in had happened. I *had* to write it down, catch the words, cement them somewhere so I wouldn't lose them.

I had spent four months slowly climbing out of a pit of emotional pain and depression. On January 1, 2000, I sat down at my computer, went to search mode on the Internet and typed in the words "narcissist" and "borderline personality disorder." A friend had told me that my partner had these disorders and that the abusive behavior being inflicted on me was … simply … because "that's what they do."

Eight hours later, still in my sweat outfit, a pile of sobbed-into tissues at my feet, I knew what the *name of my pain* was. I began to see a tiny light ahead of me to guide me out of the mess that my life had become since allowing my narcissistic, borderline personality disordered partner into my life.

What followed was a fascinating, dig-into-the-gut process of unraveling the twisted highs and lows of my relationship with my BPD (Borderline Personality Disordered) partner. I would never know when the ah-hah! moment would hit. I started carrying a small notebook with me to catch the thoughts on the spot as they came. I found myself writing in fast food restaurants, shopping malls, the post office, church – or simply at the side of the road, having pulled over in my car to quickly jot down the insights as they tumbled out.

"So *that's* why he exploded and raged at me with absolutely no warning!" "So *that's* why he withdrew and punished me with silence!" "*That's* why he wanted me home every day exactly at 5:30 p.m." The puzzle pieces of our relationship kept being arranged … and then re-arranged … the more I studied and learned about the disorder. I finally understood why he'd be so angry if I were even a little bit late … or if we had to re-arrange plans at the last minute.

I went back further and further in our relationship, shining a light into every corner, re-remembering hurtful, puzzling interactions that now had an explanation. It was exhausting, exhilarating and satisfying.

And, finally, each insight led me to a prayer … for healing, guidance, forgiveness, compassion, strength, courage and wisdom … the tools I so desperately needed to climb out of the pain.

Slowly, the insights took on character and purpose – even a sense of humor. I was healing. As I wrote, I knew the words were meant for others to read, a lifeline from me to them … reality crumbs in the forest to lead the way out.

If you're in an abusive relationship now – or even a very painful one – there is a good possibility that your partner is BPD, or some variation/combination of BPD with one of the other nine personality disorders. In the sections titled *Definitions and Behavior Descriptions* and *Resources and Tools,* you can get into your head and study the behavioral characteristics.

However, I recommend you *stay with your heart.* Don't try to understand the definitions to begin with. Dive into the meat of the book first. Connect with the feelings you have over how you've been treated, what it *feels* like. In the end, it's our feelings that will lead us to the actions we need to take to protect ourselves and our families.

My writings are in no particular order, other than chronologically as they were written. Same with Ashleigh Brilliant's illustrations. Start wherever the message grabs you and ride it to wherever it takes you.

This is an experiential book, meant to move you from one spot to another, with you in complete control of the speed and direction.

It's my sincere wish that this book will be the soul-freeing gift to others that it has been for me.

Blessings and courage, my friends. Love and happiness await you at the end of your journey.

Lynn Melville

About the Author

The author enjoys the company of her grandsons

In writing this book, Lynn's personal mission is to raise awareness of *boomerang love*, so that it becomes a household phrase, the meaning of which is clear to everyone.

She believes that repeatedly leaving and then returning to a painful relationship with another person is a sign that something is seriously wrong – we just haven't known what that *something* is.

Our culture is essentially *color blind* to the behavior of narcissistic Borderline Personality Disordered (BPD) people. Few know that there is an actual name and mental health diagnosis for the hurtful behavior that BPDs inflict on their partners in relationships. With the awareness that this book generates about BPD, Lynn hopes that families will seek professional mental health assistance sooner, both for themselves and the BPD they love.

Lynn has served as executive director of the Mental Health Association in her home town. Working with an all-volunteer board and community volunteers, she strived to educate people about mental health issues. She has also served on numerous charitable boards and with many non-profit organizations. She currently works as a long term care insurance agent and resides in the Central Coast region of California. For more information, see Lynn's web site at:

www.boomeranglove.com.

About Ashleigh Brilliant

I first met Ashleigh Brilliant in the early 1980s, when his Pot-Shots® had become so popular that he began publishing them in book form. I loved them so much that I bought every book he published.

Pot-Shots® are epigrams (definition: a short poem treating concisely, pointedly, often satirically, a single thought or event, and usually ending with a witticism). Ashleigh's epigrams are printed on post cards (thus the name Pot-Shots®), with his additional personal limitation that none can be more than 17 words in length.

From post cards, which formed the basis of a unique mail-order business, these epigrams became a syndicated newspaper feature, a series of books, and all kinds of licensed products. Astonishingly, the list of epigrams at the present time has grown to over 9,000 – and all are available to be purchased as Pot-Shot® postcards on his web site at www.ashleighbrilliant.com.

The range of Ashleigh's epigrams is amazing – from questions about time, the existence of God, chocolate (!), exercise, pets, the weather, peanut butter (!) and much, much more. You name it, he's had a *Brilliant Thought* about it that'll make you laugh or cry, and sometimes both. Ashleigh is a keenly perceptive observer of human behavior with an unusual talent for not only describing that behavior in words, but capturing its essence in his drawings.

In choosing to use Ashleigh's form of expression in *Boomerang Love*, I felt his observations were the perfect complement to my writings. Who among us who's been a BPD partner doesn't identify with wishing we could have "a speaking part in our own lives"? Or who hasn't wondered how much of our own sanity will be lost in trying to save the sanity of our BPD?

Ashleigh's epigrams captured so completely the hurtful behavior of the BPD and the tragic dilemma of their partner that I felt including them in *Boomerang Love* was crucial to the overall message of the book. I hope you enjoy Ashleigh's Pot-Shots® as much as I have.

THE CREATION OF ADAM

Michelangelo's *Creation of Adam* (painted in 1510, and located in the Vatican's Sistene Chapel) shown below depicts the moment when God "breathed" life into Adam.

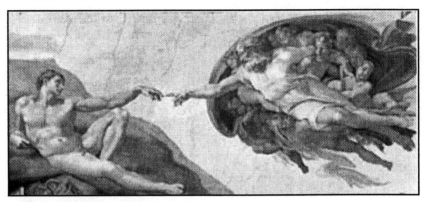

 Beside each affirmation in this book, I have used a close-up of the touching of their fingers to portray the help we receive when we request assistance from a higher power, whatever we perceive that to be.

The intimate touching of fingers also represents to me that very *human* potential of reaching out to bring hope and light into the darkness of another person's life and soul. Every spiritual master who has walked the face of our earth has called for us to love and care for one another. May we find the compassion and the humility to follow that direction.

Boomerang Love, Roller Coaster Grief and Most Valuable Dog

How do we make sense of our BPD's Dr. Jekyll and Mr. Hyde behavior? How do we order our world when it turns on a dime from peaceful to hurricane, from zero to psycho in a heartbeat? The good part, the person we love, exists right alongside (or *inside*) the hurtful one.

Whether we decide to stay and ride the BPD roller coaster – or bail out and leave the relationship – the grief is the same. We must separate from someone we love deeply.

If we stay with them, we separate emotionally. If we leave, we separate emotionally *and* physically, with all the finality and additional grief of the loss of dreams for the future, family structure, companionship, all of that.

Having to force ourselves to walk away from something we *love* is crazy-making. It flies in the face of all that's human, all that our heart wants to do, and everything that our sense of just plain *living* on this earth would have us do.

Leave someone we love? We don't do that unless *forced* to (war, famine and pestilence come to mind). It's so unnatural. Our spirits are built to pour forth love, and heaven knows our BPDs are good, deserving people. We wouldn't have chosen them to be our partners if they weren't.

But the person we *love* doesn't *stay in one place*. They move around, hiding behind walls, throwing up barriers to our intimacy, lobbing hand grenades as they run away from us. And then the person we *love* comes back ... penitent, sad, remorseful, tearful, full of promises (wishes, actually).

So back and forth we go in our grief. We're like a boomerang – catapulting ourselves out the door of our relationship and then turning around and going back through that door again. "I'm leaving him today ... but we have such a sweet love relationship ... how can I walk away from that?" Or, "I've left and he'll never rage at me again ... but I still love him ... what's wrong with me?"

1

Confusing, convoluted, roller coaster, stuck "boomerang love" grief. 12-step programs call it the "Dance of Death" – it'll kill us.

I'm reminded of a story I heard once about a man who owned two dogs. The two dogs got locked into a vicious fight, and it was clear that the owner was not going to be able to stop the fighting. The only way to stop it was to shoot one of the dogs.

He said to his friend, "I don't know what to do. These are valuable dogs. I paid a lot of money for them, and I love them both. But they're going to kill each other, so I've got to shoot one of them. Which one do I shoot?"

The friend said, "I suggest you shoot the least valuable dog."

Now, I'm not saying that our BPD partners aren't valuable. But the reality is that *we* are caught in the downward spiral of *their* disorder. It's a vortex that will suck us right down with them.

If our partners are not honestly making an effort to heal from their disorder, we have *no* choice but to choose ourselves. *We* are the most valuable dog at that point, but we are of no value to anyone – ourselves, our families or our BPD – if we allow ourselves to go down with *their* ship.

And maybe … just maybe … our walking away from the struggle and leaving them by themselves will allow them to see that their feelings arise whether we're around or not!

We *will* create lives of happiness for ourselves and our families. *We* are the most valuable dog!

 GOD, FOR TODAY help me to control my boomerang love. Help me to step over, walk around, punch my way through my grief and take care of myself in whatever way I must. And help me tomorrow, next week, next month, and next year.

BOOBY-TRAPPED LOVE

When my BPD partner laughed at my jokes, I felt as if my Dad was in the room with me. When my partner hugged me, I melted in his arms, because my Dad had loved me so fiercely. When my partner was proud of me for an accomplishment, I could hear my Dad saying, "Atta girl!" I adored my Dad and he adored me. I gave that open-wide, adoring, vulnerable, 100 per cent trusting love to my BPD partner.

However, when I had to work late for an appointment, my partner felt abandoned, as he had felt when, at age two, he lost his mother. When I tried to work with him on a project, he felt criticized if I had a different opinion, as he had felt when, later in his childhood, his mother had criticized and put him down mercilessly. Or he felt controlled, as he had felt as a child when he had no power over what would happen to him.

I thought my partner's love was open, trusting and vulnerable, like mine. Instead, it was distrustful, wary, fearful of closeness and intimacy, and invulnerable. I couldn't see it because, on the surface, he *seemed* so much like my Dad had been. He presented to me the person he *would have liked to have been,* **not** *the person he actually was.* And there's where the pain in our relationship began – for both of us.

Unbeknownst to me, the love I received from my BPD partner was booby-trapped – a step in the wrong direction and a nuclear holocaust was triggered! In order not to be hurt by the holocaust – and to try to prevent it – I learned to step carefully – the walking on egg shells routine.

Slowly, I wasn't as spontaneous as I used to be. I didn't smile and laugh as much. I became content to be glad that at least he wasn't mad at me for something. But deep, deep inside of me, I was so very sad – what professionals call *depression.*

I worked more and more, so I wouldn't have to feel. I became passive/aggressive in small ways – not doing things I knew he'd like or wanted, because I felt totally powerless to change the hurtful behavior being hurled at me without warning from out of nowhere.

Day by day, I gave myself away, *revising* my "self" into a scared little church mouse … an inch at a time … until I no longer remembered where I put my "self," or who I used to be.

I became the boob in the booby-trapped relationship, going through the motions and trying to hold it all together with bubble gum, a wish and a prayer. It didn't work, because it *couldn't* work. It wasn't enough. It would never be enough.

The only way out is with knowledge of the disorder, its symptoms and behaviors, our part in the drama, and how and where to get help. Without this, we may not survive – physically or emotionally.

GOD, FOR TODAY give me the strength to keep searching for answers, whether I stay with my BPD partner or not. Lead me to therapists who truly understand and can diagnose and treat BPD. Help me find those therapists who also understand the living hell created by this disorder for me, my partner and our family. We've all suffered long enough.

Open my heart so that I may trust that help is on the way. It's been such a long time coming … and I'm so weary.

If I go out of my mind, I'll do it quietly, so as not to disturb you.

Ashleigh Brilliant .com

The Day I Cried "Uncle"

In my own personal journey, my BPD partner, even though a highly educated professional, chose not to seek recovery.

I loved him deeply, and letting him go was one of the hardest things I've ever done.

Despite all my learning about the disorder, getting a clear snapshot of how it functioned in his head was really difficult. I had studied the *cognitive distortions* of the BPD, as they're called, and had seen them in action with my partner. But pulling it into one picture, a visual of being in his head and looking out – *seeing* the process at work, and thus truly being able to understand it – escaped me.

At a Co-Dependents Anonymous meeting one night, one of the people sharing there told what it was like for her. She talked about her "cut and run" behavior. Any time she even *felt* the person she was with *might* hurt her (abandon her) – she herself left. "FU" were her words.

She said she could deal with her fearful emotions better when by herself, and when she was alone – her weaknesses weren't apparent to others. In other words, she didn't have to admit her fears of abandonment to her partner.

Best of all, by doing the cut and run behavior *herself,* she avoided all the pain of possible abandonment – because *she* was the one doing the abandoning! And she did this abandoning behavior even though she *knew* it was only her mistaken perception that it might happen that was driving her. Whew!

She said she had no empathy for the person she was running from. If they had the *potential* to hurt her, they *deserved* the punishment she was dishing out.

She said she made them "not exist" in her mind. They were "lowly, unworthy, non-human beings." Through this mental manipulation, she could do hurtful things to others and not feel guilt, again because they "deserved" it.

She said the closer she allowed herself to be with another person, the more *power* the other person had over her (power to hurt her). Therefore, when she became close with someone and felt the fear of being abandoned, she felt utterly powerless. The way she felt "wonderfully" powerful again was to hit back hard at her partner, thinking of him as "lower than low," and abandoning *him*.

She said the downside of all this was that later there was so much pain and depression over the destruction and leaving someone she loved that it drove her deeper into her addictions.

At last I saw the BPD splitting process through a BPD's eyes. I needed that deeper understanding of how the process worked to take my hands off my BPD partner and say, "I give up."

I saw clearly that unless a BPD *honestly and actively* wants to stop destroying his life (and the others in it with him), there is absolutely no hope of a better life. Period. End of story.

I cried, "Uncle."

GOD, FOR TODAY, help me to clearly see the direction in which my life is moving. Help me have faith in *progress, not perfection* in my healing journey. Keep me alert to the signposts along the way which tell me if progress is truly occurring with my BPD.

Sometimes it feels as if I'm playing a high stakes poker game with my life. Give me the knowledge and courage to know *when to hold 'em and when to fold 'em.*

©ASHLEIGH BRILLIANT 1983.   POT-SHOTS NO. 3010.

WHY DOESN'T IT HURT YOU MORE, WHEN YOU HURT ME?

Ashleigh Brilliant .com

Alone ... and Stuck ... in Our Grief

Where do we go in the loneliness of our grief?

Months after the last severe, brutal splitting/devaluation episode from my BPD partner, it hit me – I felt like I was totally alone in a sea of grief. No one I knew understood the pain and emotional damage of being in a relationship with a BPD. So no one could grieve *with* me – or even walk along with me emotionally.

If someone in my family had died, all the rest of my family would be as heartbroken and anguished as I. But in *this* instance, their fury at my BPD knew no bounds. Feel sad about him being gone? Not on your life! Good riddance and may the devil dance on his grave.

Not to mention the shame and embarrassment of the BPD behavior. My family and friends just didn't want to even talk about it. They'd rather forget how ashamed they all were at the psychotic behavior brought into our love circle.

They looked at me with blank faces as I cried. They handed me tissues, and I saw the sadness on their faces. They were sad that they'd lost their mother to a disorder they didn't understand. They felt powerless to ease their sister's pain, all the while seething inside at the insane behavior that had slashed her so deeply ... one more time.

And I ... reeling from anger at the mistreatment, sorrowing at the misdiagnoses of his disorder by mental health professionals, struggling to climb out from under the weight of deep depression ... I was forced to walk around with a forced smile on my face, trying to hide the pain, because they didn't understand.

It felt as if there was no place of solace or comfort for me. I was surrounded by people living in another reality. They laughed, they joked, they worked, they played. Their lives moved on.

It felt as if my boat had somehow been cut adrift from the rest of humanity. I floated in my canoe, holding on tightly as my emotions hit the sides, wave after wave, looking for a safe harbor to pull into and just tend my wounds ... somehow to heal.

The only safe harbor where I felt understood was the Internet and the people on the community lists who were also dealing with BPD behavior. They, too, were being raged at for small *violations*. Their nerves were also jumpy from never knowing when they'd be attacked. They wore the same plastic smile I wore. They were as beaten down as I was, trying to figure out the *name of their pain*. Eggshells littered their lives, and they walked on tip toe as I did.

The bitter pill at the end of a non-recovered BPD relationship is that it feels as if there is nowhere to go with the pain. The *stuckness* is powerful. Acceptance that there was an illness in the relationship ... yes. Acceptance that we couldn't force our BPD to want to get well ... yes.

But closure? Where do we put the love we had (and still might have) for the good part of our BPD? We fell in love with the *good* side (mask), with Dr. Jekyll. The love still exists alongside all the pain.

A death really *has* occurred. The knowledge of the existence of BPD forces an acceptance of the death of the person as we *thought* they were – and therefore our love for the *good* person must somehow die also.

It's enough to drive us nuts. The twisted torque of these powerful emotions makes it almost impossible to finally end at a healthy spot. The wounded, *unfinishedness* hangs on for a long time.

The only answer for this kind of convoluted grief is to walk away from the whole mess, to shut down our love feelings, to squash them, to lock them in a box and throw away the key ... and the box.

It reminds me of a story my mother told about herself during the time of World War II. She was on a date with a young man and they were dancing on a crowded dance floor. During wartime, rubber was in scarce supply, so all women's panties were held up with buttons (no elastic).

Well, my mother did a quick turn on that dance floor, the button popped off, and down dropped her drawers!

She looked down at the *event over which she had no control* and did the only thing reasonable – stepped out of the problem, kicked those undies to the side of the dance floor – and kept on dancing!

And so it is with us.

When we get our love feelings for our unrecovered BPD locked into that box, it needs to be kicked to the side of *our* dance floor – while we go right on dancing through the rest of *our* lives.

It's the only way out.

We didn't cause it … we can't control it … and we can't cure it.

 GOD, FOR TODAY, guide me to the people who can comfort and support me as I struggle with this terribly destructive disorder. I want to finish the grief and begin my life dance again.

POT-SHOTS NO. 3210.

© ASHLEIGH BRILLIANT 1985.

THE EXACT LOCATION OF HELL IS NOT WELL-KNOWN,

EXCEPT TO THOSE OF US WHO'VE BEEN THERE.

Ashleigh Brilliant.com

The Brain as a Plastic Purse

How many times have we had to defend ourselves and our actions to friends and family? "How could you have taken him back? Why would you let him move back in?"

"But you don't understand … he's not well … we understand each other better now … I think we can make it."

How do we describe watching a behavioral mental disorder progressively take its course through our partner … our lives … our families? In response to the thought of living with someone with a mental problem, one of my friends said, "I don't *do* moody."

Sounds simple, doesn't it? Just don't *do* moody in our relationships – cut these people out – and everything will be fine.

But what about the illness part … the disorder part? What about the disorder that was so well hidden that we didn't know it was there until we were in so deep we couldn't get out with a simple snap of the fingers?

Some of us vowed "in sickness and in health." If our partners had come down with cancer, would we leave them? Then why would we abandon them if they become *emotionally and mentally* ill in front of us?

For the most part, the disorder is hidden and doesn't *surface* until emotional intimacy triggers it. So until *we* come into their lives, it doesn't show itself.

They have an illness that's not apparent to the naked eye. Organically, there's something very wrong with their brain – both chemically and cognitively. Unfortunately, our brains aren't like the plastic purses some women carry around – where we can see all the contents inside.

The misunderstanding, lack of education, fear and stigma surrounding mental illness still remain immense in our world.

It's still difficult for me to accept that unless my friends and family have "walked a mile in my moccasins," they'll never understand or be tolerant of my journey nor that of my former BPD partner – whether that partner ever gets well or not. In their ignorance, they'll continue to tend to look down on us and judge.

My strength comes in knowing that I'm walking a higher road than is visible to most. I'm taking the steps I need to protect myself and my family. I'm setting firm boundaries, learning all I can about the disorder, talking to a mental health professional for my support and guidance, attending support groups, caring for my physical health, and nurturing my emotional health. Doing battle with the Beast requires careful, disciplined preparation.

GOD, FOR TODAY, help me to remember that everyone is on a journey of learning and awareness here on this earth. Some of us have been thrust further ahead than others because of the circumstances in our lives. Therefore, we "walk to a different drummer."

Help me to stay in step with my journey, walking in my moccasins to the beat of the drum *I* hear. I know I will receive guidance and comfort along the way and the strength to keep walking, wherever I am being led.

©ASHLEIGH BRILLIANT 1998. SANTA BARBARA.   POT-SHOTS NO. 7724.

I'VE LOOKED ALL OVER ~

WHERE CAN I FIND SOME INNER STRENGTH?

Ashleigh Brilliant.com

Near-Death Experience of the Self, the Soul and the Spirit

The Diagnostic and Statistical Manual of Mental Disorders says:

> Borderlines seem to react strongly to factors that could pro-
> duce a feeling of loss of love or of being abandoned. The over-
> riding need to feel loved motivates borderlines to try to get
> back together with their partner after a spousal conflict. To do
> so, they try to arouse the fear of abandonment, jealousy or pity
> in their partner because they themselves fear abandonment.
> When they fear the loss of the caring person, their mood shifts
> dramatically and is frequently expressed as inappropriate and
> intense anger. They disassociate and become desperately im-
> pulsive, sometimes including psychotic rage episodes.

Living through one of these psychotic rage episodes, not to mention repeated ones, leaves us feeling like our bodies have been scorched
from the inside out. The rawness, the bleeding and feeling bruised, the
shock, horror and confusion can't be described.

They say these relationships can leave us feeling as if we've been
sucked dry ... flattened ... tire tracks on the face. It reminds me of
pictures of Mt. St. Helens in Washington when the volcano erupted –
ashes everywhere, thousands of trees lying flattened on the ground,
scorched earth. The rages annihilate everything in the BPD's path.

Actually, it feels like the closest most of us will ever come to a
near-death experience of the soul. It can almost put our lights out.

How often have we looked in the mirror, shocked at the empty,
haunted look in our eyes? How many times have we seen the people in
our 12-Step programs, just emerging from hospitalization for mental
breakdowns, suicide attempts, migraine headaches, exploding intes-
tines – struggling to overcome the aftermath of BPD behavior?

We *must* get help to understand this disorder. Our BPD *must* become motivated to stop pounding on us to control their ravaging feelings and go to therapists for help.

Unless these things happen (or we leave the relationship), there are only three ways out for us — hospitalization, mental illness or death.

GOD, FOR TODAY, help me to fight the beaten-down, worn-out feeling that comes over me each time I am blamed and raged at for the feelings of my partner. I didn't *cause* them — I only *triggered* them.

Give me strength to nurture myself, one step at a time, until I am strong enough to take larger actions, speak with a louder voice, and erect psychological barriers so I am not hurting so badly.

My self, my soul and my spirit yearn for peace and serenity, love and warmth. I must protect them so they don't die too early, leaving me walking around like a shell, hollow inside.

I, too, have a journey on this earth and much to accomplish.

I *resolve* to lock hands with other partners of BPDs, walk through the pain and the lessons, and get to the other side.

Love and light await me.

POT-SHOTS NO. 3377.

Ashleigh Brilliant .com

©ASHLEIGH BRILLIANT 1985

THE LESS ANYBODY WANTS YOU,

THE LESS VALUABLE YOU BECOME,

UNLESS YOU REALLY WANT YOURSELF.

THE BURNING CORRAL

I was listening to a Co-Dependents Anonymous tape one day, where the speaker referred to a news story she'd heard concerning a fire at a horse ranch. Evidently the fire had been fierce and had spread rapidly at a time when no one was around except one stable boy.

The fire was so hot and dangerous that the stable boy was only able to save one of the beautiful, expensive horses. He led the frightened horse out of the corral and up the hill to safety.

Suddenly, the scared horse reared up, jerking the reins out of the boy's hands. To the stable boy's horror, the horse turned around, ran down the hill and right back into the burning corral!

The news commentator said this was common behavior for horses. Even though the environment they're living in is dangerous, if you take them out of it, they become so scared that they'll run back to the *comfort* of what they feel is *home*.

Is this partially what keeps us in relationships where we keep getting hurt? Are we afraid to live on our own – or do we not have the economic power to take care of ourselves?

Does the *known* pain of our relationship somehow seem better than facing the *unknown* tasks of re-setting up our lives so we're not continually hurt?

If we're staying in a burning corral because we're afraid of being on our own, we'll never have the strength to set firm boundaries with clear consequences for not honoring them. We'll be too timid to set them – or we'll give up if our partner ignores or tramples on them.

Strengthening ourselves so we can stand alone is the beginning of our journey out of pain.

 GOD, FOR TODAY, I know that I'm not alone in my journey of self-strengthening and taking back my power. I am eager to receive Your comfort and guidance as the steps on my pathway unfold. I do not want to live in a burning corral forever.

POT-SHOTS NO. 4437.

YOU'D BE SURPRISED TO KNOW HOW MANY DIFFERENT WAYS THERE ARE TO BE HURT BY YOU.

©ASHLEIGH BRILLIANT 1988.

Ashleigh Brilliant. com

COMPROMISE AND DIGNITY

I was in church one Sunday when the pastor said, "I learned a long time ago that whatever we compromise ourselves to get, we'll lose."

I was still in the early stages of learning about BPD and was grieving over all I hadn't known over the years. Deep inside me was also a deep sense of shame and embarrassment over how much of myself I'd given away in my blanket of unknowing fog, trying to *keep the peace,* not *rock the boat,* or *wake the sleeping dragon.*

I had indeed compromised myself – my integrity, my own needs and my desires. My eternal sense of optimism (naiveté and gullibility?) said, "He didn't get enough love as a child. Surely things will get better if I just love him more."

I truly believed then, as I still believe now, that love is the strongest force on this earth. But sometimes even love isn't enough.

I compromised myself and lost the relationship anyway, getting beaten up verbally as he raged out the door one more time.

Be careful, friends. Keep those boundaries firm. The emotional cost of compromise is devastating.

GOD, FOR TODAY, help me to walk the tightrope of my relationship, giving support where it's needed, love when it's accepted. Help me to see when my actions will compromise my integrity and leave me with that telltale sense of shame. I deserve to emerge from these life lessons with my dignity intact.

MY STRATEGY

IS, WHENEVER POSSIBLE, TO KEEP OUT OF THE ARENA.

SURRENDER

The more I learned about BPD, the more I felt an internal, "Uncle – I give up." I felt like one of those wooden bead toy figures that are held tightly together by string. When we push the button underneath their wooden stand, all the toy pieces, once held so snugly, relax and fall into a jumbled heap. I felt like an overcooked noodle – limp and numb with knowledge.

I finally accepted the reality of the disorder that had invaded my world. I surrendered.

It wasn't until then that I realized how tight and tense I was inside, how hard I was working to find a pathway so my partner and I could be happy again.

In the surrender, I *knew* – to the core of my being – that I could do *absolutely nothing* to heal my partner. Only *my partner* could do it … *if* he wanted to.

I felt as if I'd been the wife in the movie *Gaslight*. The husband plays tricks on her and deceives her, trying to break her down mentally so he can divorce her.

The dual worlds of BPD had been eating away at my sanity. At a moment's notice, BPDs can switch to a personal, inner reality that doesn't fit at all with what's really happening in the real world. Anger, projection and blame jump out of utterly nowhere – like monkeys flying out of trees in *The Wizard of Oz*. Zero to psycho in 30 seconds!

And then later the BPD says he wasn't angry … or didn't say what you remember him saying … or accuses you of memory deficiencies … or claims you said things you didn't say … and so on.

How does the partner of a BPD defend and protect against gaslighting like that? Sometimes we become sicker than they are – obsessively, frantically trying to find the answers to make the feelings of pain and confusion – and what feels like our own personal brand of insanity – go away.

The good news is: *We can relax now.* We've found the answer. We've learned about the BPD. We've learned what it is and how it acts. We can finally let go – release – and stop holding our breath.

GOD, FOR TODAY, help me to turn my partner over to you for recovery. I've tried so hard to be the healer. I can stop working at it now. I can surrender to the knowledge of BPD and the freedom that brings. In surrendering, I win back my "self."

© ASHLEIGH BRILLIANT 1985.

POT- SHOTS NO. 3204.

HOW MUCH MUST I CHANGE TO SATISFY YOU? ~

AND WOULD ANYTHING BE LEFT OF THE ORIGINAL ME?

© ASHLEIGH BRILLIANT 1983.

POT- SHOTS NO. 2770.

BY WHAT PROCESS DID I BECOME A STRANGER IN MY OWN LIFE?

Stop Blaming Yourself for Feeling Tricked

For a long time, I felt as if I'd been tricked. I thought my BPD partner was perfect – an independent person who could stand on his own two feet, could cook and clean, sew buttons – you name it, he could do it. At last I had an equal partner. And, of course, the sweet love relationship was the icing on the cake.

Then where in the world did the absolute, out-of-nowhere flaming rage come from? It felt like someone threw a hand grenade at my feet. *What* was *that?*

The chemical imbalance in the brain and the twisted thinking of the BPD can't be *seen* – except through those unexpected, painful eruptions. The disorder peeks to the surface in behavior that seems inappropriate to the moment.

For those of us who don't *do* that behavior, we sometimes give them excuses or minimize the hurt when it first happens. We tell ourselves, "Well, he's had a bad day at work … he doesn't feel well … his feelings were hurt," etc.

We see *their* behavior and interpret it as if it were *our* behavior. When *we* act in a similar way, we *have* had a bad day or don't feel well. It's impossible for us to imagine that their reasons for acting that way are much deeper, not healthy and in truth are only the tip of the iceberg of much, much more going on inside them.

With us, that's all that's going on – nothing deeper.

This is the reason we're all so surprised when someone goes "postal" (now a familiar term in our country for someone who shoots and kills people who they feel have been hurting them). How many times have we read newspaper articles where the neighbors say, "But he was such a nice, quiet person"?

Been there, done that. Got the t-shirt. Got the bumper sticker. Welcome to our lives.

The truth is, there was no way we could have known what was there until it was revealed. BPD behavior is triggered through *personal relationships with us – through intimacy.* Most of the time, they function in a manner that looks perfectly normal in the outside world. Go figure.

One reason they're frequently on the way out the door is that their relationship with *us* triggers the feelings and then the actions. If the BPD lives alone, the feelings, and thus the behavior, are not triggered. What a concept.

Once we understand the disorder, we can stop blaming ourselves for getting into a relationship that was full of so much torment and suffering.

Once we've done this, we can concentrate on what we need to do to help make the relationship better (*if* our BPD is actively seeking help) – or, if not, figure out how the heck to get out of it.

 GOD, FOR TODAY, help me to forgive myself for having walked into such a painful relationship. I know there's a very good part to my partner, and that's the person I love. I have beaten myself up inside mercilessly for having made what looks like such a stupid mistake.

I went into the relationship with my *heart* wide open. Help me now to fully activate my *head* to stop blaming myself and begin taking the steps necessary to protect myself and my family.

ASHLEIGH BRILLIANT 1985.

POT-SHOTS NO. 3470.

Ashleigh Brilliant.com

I WANT TO TAKE HOLD OF REALITY~ BUT SOMEBODY KEEPS MOVING IT.

Face the Direction the Horse Is Going

One of the things that keeps us *stuck* is the memory of how good things were in the past with our Jekyll and Hyde partner. The Dr. Jekyll part is *so* wonderful – more than we could have ever wished for.

BPDs connect with the people they love in a very intense manner. The high of the relationship is sweet indeed. But the high of the good side is an indication of how deeply painful the down side can be. The higher we fly on the good side, the more intense and destructive will be the crash on the down side.

When they split us and devalue us, the shock and pain are indescribable.

In order to face and deal effectively with the destructive side, we must force ourselves to accept the possibility of having to give up the precious love we so treasure. Accepting the *possibility* of this frees us to take action.

For our own health and survival, we cannot continue to look backwards at how *good* they were – or forwards to what we *hope* they will be in the future.

Reality means *what is* … and all we *have* is the reality of what they're doing to us *right now*.

I've spent much of my life either denying what's happening or believing things will get better in the future – *terminal optimism*. A friend once said to me, "Turn around and face the direction the horse is going!"

I saw this vision of myself – sitting on a horse backwards, flailing away like crazy and digging my heels into its flanks, urging it forward in the direction I'm facing. But the horse is still going where *it's* going … and *I* am going backwards! What a picture!

No matter how hard we work to make something turn out the way we want, I know *now* that most of life is out of our control. We only make it harder on ourselves when we fight it.

My Dad used to say that we need to learn to "roll with the punches" – "bend with the wind." How right you were, Dad. How right you were.

GOD, FOR TODAY, help me to let go of my need to minimize the reality of my pain. Help me to see my situation clearly – to see *what is*. I know that when I have the courage to admit *what is*, my eyes will be opened to a pathway of healing, one step at a time. Help me be receptive to the guidance in store for me.

© ASHLEIGH BRILLIANT 1990.

POT-SHOTS NO. 5221.

TO FIND OUT WHERE YOU ARE,

IT IS SOMETIMES NECESSARY TO GO SOMEWHERE ELSE.

Ashleigh Brilliant.com
SANTA BARBARA

© ASHLEIGH BRILLIANT 1995. Ashleigh Brilliant SANTA BARBARA. POT-SHOTS NO. 6606.

HOW WRONG MUST THINGS GET,

BEFORE THEY'RE WORTH ALL THE TROUBLE OF TRYING TO GET RIGHT?

R2D2

I used to mumble to myself about my BPD partner, "He should have come with an instruction book, a 24-hour interpreter, and a built-in warning system." Without those, how was I supposed to know how to stay out of the danger zones? Such a book would have told me:

- "Do not scowl at this machine or say critical words to it. That may cause it to explode."
- "When this machine says *you're* feeling a certain way, it means *it's* feeling that way."
- "This machine will do impulsive, even hurtful behaviors and then blame them on the owner. This is just how the machine is programmed. It cannot be changed."
- "This machine makes loud, unpredictable noises when provoked. And it's provoked easily over seemingly trivial issues. Try to ignore the loud noises and hope they go away."
- "After unpredictable, hurtful behavior, this machine will not apologize. Empathy and compassion programs were not installed on its hard drive."

Or the R2D2 interpreter:

- "My master doesn't really mean *you're* a controlling person. He means *he* feels powerless most of the time and fearful of asking for what he wants."
- "My master doesn't really feel the family is going bankrupt. He suffers from a deep fear of financial insecurity and any little thing can set the fear off."
- "My Master wants intimacy, but just the right amount. Don't come too close and don't go too far away. Maintaining this careful balance will assure that the machine functions properly."

And the dream of all dreams – the built-in warning system:

- "WARNING! WARNING! This machine will begin loud, self-destructive acts within the next few minutes. You must leave the area immediately! I repeat, you MUST vacate the premises immediately!!"

My great-grandmother used to say, "If wishes were horses, then beggars would ride."

GOD, FOR TODAY, help me keep a sense of humor about the predicament I'm in.

The humorist and essayist C. W. Metcalf said, "Humor is about perspective – a willingness to access joy even in adversity."

©ASHLEIGH BRILLIANT 1992.   POT-SHOTS NO. 5996.

GOING BERSERK AND RUNNING AMOK

ARE SIMPLY MY WAY OF COPING WITH THINGS.

POT-SHOTS NO. 4855.   ©ASHLEIGH BRILLIANT 1989.

SOME PEOPLE SHOULD BE REQUIRED TO WEAR WARNING-SIGNS.

DANGER

Ashleigh Brilliant.com
SANTA BARBARA

Perspective on the Journey

(Most Valuable Dog Revisited)
A poem by Mary Oliver

The Journey

One day you finally knew
what you had to do, and began,
though the voices around you
kept shouting their bad advice –
though the whole house
began to tremble
and you felt the old tug at your ankles.
"Mend my life!" each voice cried.
But you didn't stop.
You knew what you had to do,
though the wind pried with its stiff fingers
at the very foundations,
though their melancholy was terrible.
It was already late enough, and a wild night,
and the road full of fallen branches and stones.
But little by little,
as you left their voices behind,
the stars began to burn through the sheets of clouds,
and there was a new voice
which you slowly recognized as your own,
that kept you company as you strode
deeper and deeper into the world,
determined to do
the only thing you could do –
determined to save
the only life you could save.

GOD, FOR TODAY, help me to listen to the quiet voice inside me which is offering comfort and guidance through all the noise and confusion of my life. Give me the ears to hear … the eyes to see … and the courage to follow through.

I must remember that *I am the most valuable dog*.

©ASHLEIGH BRILLIANT 1985.   POT-SHOTS NO. 3352

Where I come from and where I belong are not necessarily the same place.

©ASHLEIGH BRILLIANT 1980   POT-SHOTS NO. 1726.

UNLESS YOU MOVE,

THE PLACE WHERE YOU ARE IS THE PLACE WHERE YOU WILL ALWAYS BE.

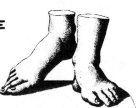

THE THREE A's: AWARENESS, ACCEPTANCE, ACTION

The process of dealing with the problems that have surfaced in my life seems to have followed what I now call *The Three A's*. Each is a steppingstone that *must* be stepped on in order to reach the solution to the problem.

First comes *awareness*. One day I'm happy with my life, things are moving along as I'd like – and then boom! … a doubting thought creeps into my head … or an uncomfortable feeling sweeps over me. What was *that?*

Is he really telling the truth? Is my job as secure as I think it is? Can I trust my spouse/co-worker/relative? Why do I feel so uneasy? Or maybe I've been hurt deeply by someone I trusted and loved. I'm beginning to slowly become *aware* of something not … quite … right … in my life.

My first inclination is to minimize the thought or feeling, shove it down, talk myself out of it. (Mental health professionals call this denial or repression.)

Denial is a warm blanket we wrap around ourselves, cocooning us from the pain of knowledge of the truth about our lives.

If what we're denying is real, though, it'll keep coming back. The hurts will continue, the doubting thoughts will recur … and they'll fly in our face ever larger until we're ready to drop our warm blanket and move to the next steppingstone – *acceptance*.

I have found this to be the hardest step. If I accept that my job is insecure, I should take steps to get another one that *is* secure. If someone continues to hurt me, I should confront them about it. I must find a way out of the *deer in the headlights* syndrome. I may have to find the courage to move this person out of my life so I don't continue to be hurt.

Acceptance will require that I move to the third steppingstone – *action*. But fear has many times kept me tippy-toed and trapped on steppingstone two.

In my journey, I've found that the acceptance stage will lead me through all the five stages of grief. I go through *shock* and *denial* as I first become aware of the problem. As I struggle with *acceptance* (sometimes feels like trying to swallow a whale), I swing back and forth between *depression* and *anger*.

I have a friend who says, "The truth will set you free ... but first it's going to tick you off!"

Acceptance finally crawls out at the end, dragging me with it.

For those of us struggling to accept the reality of the BPD disorder in our lives, there's another step that will lead us to acceptance. That's *education and knowledge.*

What we're struggling to accept isn't as simple as whether or not our job is secure or if we should sell our home and move to a residence that better fits our income. BPD is cunning and crafty. It hides cleverly and then reveals itself in hundreds of different ways, none of which we understand without education about the disorder. Not knowing about BPD, we're like a person who's color blind. How can we see the color red?

We're left feeling as if we've been spun in a circle blindfolded and then told to "Pin the Tail on the Problem." How do we find something that we've never known existed? It's like playing hide-and-seek with a ghost who knows all the hiding places.

We're not given the name of the ghost, what it looks like, how it acts or sounds, *or* a map of the places where it might hide! Yet in order to bring peace to our lives – or at the very least, stop the ongoing pain we're experiencing – we have to find that ghost.

It becomes a grand detective game played for life's most precious possessions – physical health, mental health and spiritual wellbeing.

It's a high stakes poker game. With no knowledge or education about BPD, we can't win. We have no chips.

 GOD, FOR TODAY, give me the courage to stop denying the reality of what I'm living with and the willingness to accept my place at the poker table. I know that acceptance is the key to the action of acquiring knowledge about BPD.

Each piece of education I receive represents another poker chip on my side of the table. As the stacks grow, I'll play the game more skillfully. Ultimately, I'll know whether I want to continue playing the game – or take my chips and move on.

IT'S NOT ABOUT YOU — IT'S ABOUT YOUR PARTNER

There's a big difference between working through our grief and taking things personally.

Your partner has a mental disorder — how can *you* be responsible for his/her behavior? The rages? The blaming? The leaving? The affairs? The physical violence?

If we had planned to take a walk and a thunderstorm happened, would we feel responsible if we got hit by lightning? Or would it be our fault if our garage flooded from the rain?

Of course we wouldn't blame ourselves for a lightning storm — it's beyond our control. But that's what we do when the BPD's actions are hurled at us.

We spend years believing we caused and brought on the lightning, when in fact, we're just the lightning *rod* — it's attracted to us! We didn't *cause* their behavior — we just *triggered* it.

It's ... not ... our ... fault.

 GOD, FOR TODAY, help me not be so hard on myself. Help me not be so quick to take the blame when my BPD rages. I am *not* responsible for *everything* that happens in this world.

POT-SHOTS No. 2413.

YESTERDAY,
        UPON MY BACK,
YOUR BURDEN
    SUDDENLY
        APPEARED ~

HOW DID
YOU DO IT?

Ashleigh
Brilliant
.com

RELATIONSHIP AS A CANCELABLE CONTRACT

To a BPD, a relationship is sometimes just a contract … a *cancelable* one … at *their* control and whim.

Dr. Sam Vaknin, originator of the NPD Central website (www.geocities.com/vaksam), which focuses on narcissistic personality disorder, says:

> Whoever might require my services can be my "partner." I provide intelligence, money, insight, fun, good company, status, and so on. I "expect" narcissistic supply (attention, adoration) in return. The contract runs its natural course until it is "terminated," as do all "business contracts."

When I read this, I hear my BPD partner's words of wanting "reciprocity" in our marriage, and how we were "incompatible." I never understood those words … felt so confused and hurt. I freely gave my love, not expecting anything *specific* in return. If he were grouchy or withdrawn, I assumed he'd had a rough day and believed he would return to his old self, who I loved.

When *I* was grouchy or withdrawn, however, I see now that I was violating the relationship "contract." If I wasn't available for a long enough period of time to meet his nonverbalized needs, he was free to terminate the contract, raging at me, "It's all your fault!" as he headed out the door.

He "cancelled" our "contract."

 GOD, FOR TODAY, help me to choose wisely in my relationships next time … if there *is* a next time. Guide me to a relationship where I am free to be myself, warts and all – a relationship where I'm free to have a *time out* of giving (during a physical illness, a deep grieving over the death of a loved one) without being punished.

I want a relationship where my partner is able to step forward in *my* time of need to lovingly care for *me*. I am a good, caring person. I deserve to receive the kind of love that I offer.

© ASHLEIGH BRILLIANT 1988.

POT-SHOTS NO. 4712.

WHENEVER I'M ALONE WITH YOU,

WHY DO I ALWAYS FEEL OUTNUMBERED?

Ashleigh Brilliant.com

It's Not Our Fault, It's Not Our Fault, It's Not Our Fault

No matter how many times we're told by outside parties that we're not to blame for our BPD's behavior, it's hard not to accept those accusations when they're hurled at us like swords.

We said something innocently, asked a question, needed some help, *wished* for something (God forbid!) – whatever – and an absolute *hurricane* of psychotic rage is slung at us. We're devastated, flattened to the wall, battered and bruised inside.

What did we do? What did we say? Was it our tone of voice? Did we imply something? We turn ourselves inside out trying to figure out what in the *world* could have caused such fury. How *could* he have gotten so angry over something so trivial?

Their behavior doesn't make sense, makes us crazy trying to figure it out, and our spirits bleed inside. Yet we *try* to figure it out, because it's so painful that we don't want it to ever happen again. We're trying desperately to prevent it.

The truth is, *they* don't know why they do it, either. They're less in touch with reality than *we* are. But according to them, since *we* said something that triggered an emotion with *them, we* must be at fault – *we* caused it.

Both parties are groping in the dark, looking for a way out of the pain. The problem is: *both parties blame the same person – us!* One of us needs to stop the blame cycle and get off the merry-go-round.

GOD, FOR TODAY, help me to remember that *I* didn't cause this disorder (may those who *did* cause it suffer an equal consequence, thank you very much). I can't control it (trying to stop a raging BPD is like throwing feathers at a stampeding rhinoceros). And *I* certainly can't cure it (although *they* can work at controlling it – and recovering from it – if they *choose*).

Help me to stop beating myself up about something over which I have *absolutely no control.*

POT-SHOTS NO. 1145.

THE SHOW MUST GO ON

BUT
I DON'T HAVE TO
STAY AND WATCH!

Ashleigh
Brilliant.com

©BRILLIANT ENTERPRISES 1977.

BOTTOM LINES FOR BPD PARTNERS

As partners of a BPD, it isn't possible for us to get the relationship we want from a person who is:

- Undiagnosed but obviously has problems working in a relationship
- Not in treatment for whatever issues they have that stop their ability to function in close relationships
- A diagnosed BPD who is unwilling to seek treatment.

Nothing we do or say, no threats we make, no trying to take charge, will change the reality of the above. These actions will only trigger a BPD reaction.

BPD is a mental disorder, and we cannot change the misfiring signals of their brains or give them the chemicals they need to stop the overreactions. We're not capable of reprogramming them, no matter how much we believe *love* will do it.

So if we stick around with them, the only way things *might* get a little better is to set boundaries to protect ourselves. Then we let them go through whatever hell they're going to create in their own way.

Whether or not we go through the hell *with* them is *our* decision — the *only* one we have.

 GOD, FOR TODAY, help me to think clearly. What would I do if my partner had a heart condition yet still ate fatty foods and wouldn't exercise? How would I react if he had diabetes and wouldn't stop eating sugar? Eventually, I'd have to get out of his way and let the consequences of his actions happen to him ... *without* putting a pillow under his tush when he hits bottom.

Help me to remember that my partner is ill, but I can't save him from the results of his actions. If he continues to do the actions which I have said will have consequences to them, give me the strength to follow through on those consequences.

Help me to get off his back, out of his way, and on with my life.

POT-SHOTS NO. 2446

If you tire of your dreams, REALITY IS ALWAYS AVAILABLE AT NO EXTRA CHARGE.

© ASHLEIGH BRILLIANT 1982.

I Can't Change Anyone (But Sometimes I Wish To)

How many psychiatrists does it take to change a light bulb? Only one – but the light bulb has to really want to change.

And so it is with BPD. No one can change another person who doesn't want to change.

However, BPD is not a complete, full-blown psychosis. It's a personality *dis*-order. It's horrible, painful, and hurts the sufferer and everyone who cares about them. But there are long periods with BPDs where they are aware of right and wrong – and have a *knowing* that something is not right with them.

BPD denial is one of the biggest enemies. Strong boundaries (behaviors we will not tolerate) on our part are the only way to counteract it.

It's true we can't make someone *do* anything like therapy. But we *can* encourage our BPDs to question why they're doing things, tell them we don't accept those reasons, and let them know their behavior is unacceptable, along with the consequences that will befall them if they continue that behavior.

What they *do* with that knowledge is then up to them.

 GOD, FOR TODAY, help me to accept that I can't change anyone. Help me to remember that advice or help not asked for is usually not taken. Show me how to accept myself as I am ... impossible wishes, dreams and all.

I promise to keep taking care of myself by setting clear boundaries with my BPD. I know that all things change, end, move on – as will my BPD relationship. I don't know what the future holds, but my goal is to be a whole person when the dust settles – not road-kill.

POT-SHOTS NO. 4858.

© ASHLEIGH BRILLIANT 1989.

HOW MUCH MORE MUST I INVEST IN THIS RELATIONSHIP,

BEFORE I GET BACK ANYTHING WORTH HAVING?

Ashleigh Brilliant.com
SANTA BARBARA

SETTING AND ENFORCING BOUNDARIES

As partners of people with BPD, we must set boundaries (actions we will not allow them to take against us, lines we will not allow them to cross) and stick with them for our *own* sake. We must *enforce* those boundaries (set consequences if they violate those limits) – again, for *ourselves.*

This is not so much about changing who the BPD person is as much as it's about letting them know what is *not* acceptable … for the sake of *our* survival.

If our BPD is functional enough, he then has the choice to change and conform – or lose the relationship. Ball in his court. End of story.

Ultimately, we *are* in control of ourselves, even with a BPD partner. If we weren't, it wouldn't be possible for *anyone* to ever get better, ourselves included.

GOD, FOR TODAY, help me remember that my first responsibility is to myself. I *must* survive this. I must protect my children. I must figure out how I got into a relationship like this … and find a way to survive it or get out of it … with my sanity and body intact.

Mending my heart, soul and spirit will take a little longer ….

POT-SHOTS NO. 4027.

© ASHLEIGH BRILLIANT 1987.

IT'S SURPRISING HOW FAR YOU CAN GO THROUGH LIFE

WITHOUT EVER HAVING WHAT YOU REALLY NEED.

How Did This Happen? How Did My Sweet Love Relationship Get So Bad?

"How did this happen?" Boiled down to its essence, the answer is simple – I tried to have an intimate relationship with someone who's incapable of intimacy – for whatever reason.

He *tried*. He watched the moves and actions of others and imitated them. I didn't know they were imitations – efforts at being *real*.

Since I believed they *were* real (backed by true emotions and feelings), when the bizarre overreactions began, I couldn't figure them out. They didn't fit with who I thought my partner was. I kept sharing in my 12-Step meetings that, "I *can't* get these two people rectified in my mind."

I was confused, hurt, angry, and *very* puzzled. I began to have names for the *other personality:* Hunk Rah (fire-breathing character in Doonesbury cartoons); Mr. Hyde; and finally, in a sense of resignation, just George (not my partner's name) – as in, "Oh, George is back," and then simply, "Hi, George."

When I tried to come close and connect with my partner in an intimate way, he'd push me away, lock the door on his emotions and accuse me of mothering him, or controlling him.

When I pulled away, hurt that my love offerings were rebuffed, he felt abandoned by me.

I was damned if I did, and damned if I didn't.

Knowledge of the disorder clears the view and makes the confusion understandable. It doesn't make the hurt go away, but it's no longer necessary to hurt in silence and bewilderment.

There are therapists now who are trained to diagnose and treat BPD. This book and others can help us cope with the disorder, so we don't get physically or mentally ill ourselves. Internet mailing lists give us friends to cry with and learn new coping strategies.

It may be painful to be in a BPD relationship, but at least the disorder is finally coming out of the closet. For that we can be thankful. Progress is slowly being made.

GOD, FOR TODAY, help me to know that I don't have to go it alone anymore … hanging my head in shame and humiliation, accepting blame that isn't mine. Give me the courage to step forward, admit the pain in my life, and ask for help. It's there for the asking now.

©ASHLEIGH BRILLIANT 1982.   POT-SHOTS NO. 2406.

MY
GREAT
AMBITION
IS
TO SECURE
A
SPEAKING PART
IN
MY OWN LIFE.

Ashleigh Brilliant .com

©ASHLEIGH BRILLIANT 1996. SANTA BARBARA.   POT-SHOTS NO. 7088.

WHY AM I
SO EASILY
DECEIVED

BY
PEOPLE
WHO TELL ME
WHAT I DESPERATELY
WANT TO BELIEVE?

Ashleigh Brilliant .com

ADDICTIVE RELATIONSHIPS, LINES IN THE SAND AND QUACKING DUCKS

I've never quite understood the term *addictive relationship*. I know I couldn't stop going back to my BPD partner after being hurt by him, couldn't stop trying to figure out what *I* was doing to cause *his* behavior (riding in on my white horse, to rescue and fix things, of course).

But addiction? Really, now. I worked a good job, joined clubs, had friends. *Addicts* needed more and more drugs and alcohol – and their lives got to be a mess. Not so with me.

As I began my recovery journey in Adult Children of Alcoholics, Al-Anon and Co-Dependents Anonymous, I began to look at my behaviors of people-pleasing, placating, and caretaking, with fear of abandonment and fear of anger mixed in.

I saw where these behaviors were sabotaging my life, preventing me from drawing lines in the sand that said, "These behaviors are hurtful and unacceptable."

And my life was okay for a while. What I didn't understand was that my sabotaging traits are deeply-ingrained *survival* behaviors for me. The very life of my spirit *depended* on these behaviors to *survive* in my childhood home.

So, I can stay in control of myself and not self-sabotage under routine circumstances. But put me anywhere near someone who *might* blow up in anger or rage, and I freeze like the proverbial opossum caught on the back yard fence in the porch light. Help!! How do I disappear myself? I can no more draw a line in the sand than fly to the moon. I *must* placate and people-please. I *must* calm the angry beast-person – so the fear pounding in my chest will go away.

I am an absolute, scared-out-of-my-mind, *quacking sitting duck* for someone who uses anger to intimidate and manipulate others to get their way.

This is where *addicted* fits for me. I *have* to do the behavior. I have no choice. The fear in me demands it.

And it's a vicious, downward cycle – just like drugs and alcohol. The angry behavior *works* on me, so it's done again. And again I grovel, dipping deeper, inch-by-inch giving up parts of myself. I hate myself for doing it, but I can't stop. The fear is all-consuming. It's like a merry-go-round that I can't get off. And my life gets to be a *mess*.

The answer is the same as for any addiction – stay away from the addictive substance.

For me, that means staying away from people who aren't safe – people who scare me – people I'm afraid of – people who manipulate others through temper tantrums, rage and sarcasm – people who must have their own way or they withdraw their love or punish.

Any of these behaviors shrink me all the way back to a scared little girl.

If I don't have the strength to stand up to these people, then I need to make *darned* sure I don't let them into my life.

 GOD, FOR TODAY, help me to surround myself with *safe* people – friends, acquaintances, work environments, bosses, family members and especially lovers and spouses. People who scare me will endanger my "sobriety" (will cause me to people-please), my sanity and my very physical well-being. They'll lure me to drink of the cup of self-sabotaging fear again. I don't want to slip again.

I've waited so long to feel safe. I don't want my life to be a *mess* ever again.

POT-SHOTS NO. 4575.

THE ONLY
WAY OUT
OF SOME
TROUBLES

IS
NEVER TO
GET INTO THEM.

©ASHLEIGH BRILLIANT 1988.   Ashleigh Brilliant.com

Intellectual Acceptance vs. Emotional Acceptance

When we first discover the disorder of BPD, it's such a relief. We *knew* something was wrong – *very, very* wrong – in our BPD relationship but just couldn't put our finger on it.

We couldn't figure out why we could say something one day and get one reaction and then have much the same interaction another day with a totally different, very upsetting reaction from them.

It didn't make sense.

Such relief. *Now* we have an answer. *Now* we can go to work on it – learn all about it, determine our part in it and what we need to change. We can learn new methods of interacting, hoping to help the BPD heal … or at least avoid the triggers that cause the behavior that hurts *us* so much.

Intellectual acceptance comes first and takes a number of months to absorb. It's the honeymoon time, the *hope* period.

Out of the blue, we're hit by the next stage – emotional acceptance. We realize this is not an illness that's going to go away quickly. It's going to take a lot of work on the part of our BPD to even *begin* to see improvement.

There is no antibiotic to *cure* it. There are antidepressants and mood stabilizers, but their effectiveness depends on a good prescribing doctor and a BPD *willing* to be medication-compliant. And then, in order to be truly effective, there's the many years of cognitive therapy needed after that.

If the BPD is unable to *see* the illness as theirs, the usual reaction is to blame *us* for their overwhelming feelings. Then they say they don't want to be a *sick* person who needs medicine. And they're certainly not receptive to any kind of therapy.

So we begin to see that this is going to be a long haul – with many peaks and valleys – and no guaranteed outcome.

It takes a while for the truth to really sink in. We know we're there when the grief hits. Sometimes it's hard and heavy, intense with tears. We feel trapped.

Other times we push the acceptance down. It's too hard to look at our lives and our future, now fully knowing the Beast and the battle ahead. We don't want to get out of bed … we eat when we're not hungry … we need to comfort ourselves … it feels overwhelming.

Hope seems to have moved to *hopeless*.

Now is the time to practice our 12-Step tools. None of us knows what the future holds. If we try to look too far down the road, we can feel overwhelmed. Taking our existence *one day at a time* helps to bring a sense of control back into our lives. We can do something just for today that would overwhelm us if we thought we had to do it for the rest of our lives.

Let go and let God enables us to take a deep breath and accept that we can't know everything about how the future will work out. We hand it over to a power greater than ourselves to handle for us … and then go do the laundry.

There's a balance and an order to our lives that we can only see when looking backwards. Whether or not we stay in the relationship with our BPD , we can have faith that we will be guided on that path. We will be provided with the answer when we need it.

GOD, FOR TODAY, help me to silence my fears and anxieties. I know that the disorder of BPD took many years to form and that it won't go away overnight. I ask for wisdom to know what I need to do to protect myself and my family and to help my BPD. And most of all, I ask for *strength* to carry out those actions.

©ASHLEIGH BRILLIANT 1983.

POT-SHOTS NO. 2360.

SOMETIMES
MY MIND
IS SO
UNCOMFORTABLE,

I WISH
I COULD
GO SOMEWHERE
AND
TAKE IT OFF.

Ashleigh Brilliant.com

BLACK AND WHITE LOVE – HE LOVES ME, HE LOVES ME NOT

Professionals call it *object constancy*. It's the ability to retain within ourselves the memory of the love we have for another person and their love for us. It's also our *internal* knowledge of the person we love – who they are when they're happy, when they're sad, when they're angry, and all the shades of gray behavior in between.

A person who can maintain object constancy can experience their loved one's absence and still feel loved by them. They can see them withdraw in grief over the death of a friend or relative and still feel loved by them. Even in the midst of an argument, they know they are loved and that their partner will return to his or her regular self after the heat of battle is over.

BPDs can't do that.

When we withdraw to grieve over something in our lives, BPDs feel abandoned and unloved. When we leave for a business trip, go to take care of an ill relative or just take some time away, they again feel abandoned and unloved.

When we have a disagreement with them, they not only feel unloved and abandoned but also criticized and put down … even if we just want canned tomatoes in the soup!

As horrifying as it may sound, *BPDs judge the quality of our relationships with them based on the last interaction we had with them.*

I repeat – *BPDs judge the quality of our relationships with them based on the last interaction we had with them.*

If it was good (we cooked a good meal, hugged them, brought them a surprise gift, had satisfying lovemaking), then they perceive the relationship to be good.

If it was bad (had some anger in it, we were distracted or impatient, our feelings got hurt, we left on a business trip without giving them a hug, whatever), then *that* becomes the sum total of the BPD's perception of our relationship.

This starts the BPD process call *splitting*. First we're on a pedestal and the love we receive from them is stars in the nighttime sky. We couldn't be happier.

Then we have a mild disagreement over something trivial, and we're thrown in the trash can. Without warning, they're rude, sarcastic, blaming, downright mean and punishing – if not raging out the door.

They *split* us *all bad* or *all good*. They can't maintain their own internal balance (object constancy), as they're flooded with painful overreactions to *perceived* slights. We're either incredibly wonderful – or the scum of the earth. There's no middle ground for us in their internal perceptions.

They live in a black and white world, making mountains out of molehills ("pole-vaulting over rat turds," as they say in Alcoholics Anonymous). Black and white love – he loves me – he loves me not. They run, throwing lighted sticks of dynamite at us as they head out the door.

Whew! And this is our *love* relationship? Understanding and dealing with this aspect of BPD-ness is the most difficult of all because of its *kicked-in-the-gut, rug-pulled-out-from-under-us* feeling.

Our first instinct is to kick back ... hard (guess where?). That only makes it worse.

If our BPD is actively working to recover from the disorder, then learning the "SET" method of interacting in the book *I Hate You – Don't Leave Me* by Dr. Jerold Kreisman and Hal Straus is helpful. Also useful is the "PUVAS" method in *Stop Walking on Eggshells* by Paul Mason and Randi Kreger.

Also vital are setting boundaries (behaviors we will *not* tolerate) and enforcing them. Attending all the 12-Step programs we can find for support is important. And don't forget loving self-nurturance.

Most important is not allowing ourselves to be "sleepwalkers." Sleepwalking through our lives by allowing denial or minimizing to slip into our perceptions will only lead us to more pain. Staying alert to whether or not the hurtful behavior is truly diminishing is *crucial*. It's information we need in order to make decisions in *our* lives for *us*.

GOD, FOR TODAY, I ask for the courage and strength to hold up against the BPD onslaught when I am split "all bad." Help me find ways to protect myself as the healing and recovery process continues with my partner.

© ASHLEIGH BRILLIANT 1985. POT-SHOTS NO. 3438.

THE THINGS I'M PRAYING FOR

SOMETIMES MATTER LESS THAN THE THINGS I'M PRAYING AGAINST.

POT-SHOTS NO. 903.

I'LL BE GLAD
WHEN IT'S ALL OVER,

AND I CAN
TAKE MY SMILE OFF.

© BRILLIANT ENTERPRISES 1976

Ashleigh
Brilliant
.com

MOVING TARGET DEFENSE

Before I found out about BPD, the only way I could protect myself from the confusing pain that came out of nowhere from my partner was to avoid it. I would dodge, duck, try to be invisible, hide, look the other way, repress my feelings, deny my feelings, smile a lot ("happy" face), pretend and stay busy (*very* busy). I just instinctively did anything I could to dodge the bullets. They say it's hard to shoot a moving target ....

What I really needed was a Star Wars type of invisible shield around me to deflect the slings and arrows of the disorder. This is what education about the disorder does for us. It shields us and deflects our pain from the blaming, projection and rage ... or at least the hurt doesn't penetrate in as far. With practice and more education, we can learn to not let it in at all.

Of course, there's a danger in being so safely shielded and protected from our partner. Along the way, we can lose the love we have for them and be left feeling nothing but pity and apathy. This is why it's so important to continue watching whether they're taking the steps necessary to heal. If they are, we'll be able to slowly lower the shield. If they aren't, the slow loss of our love for them will at least finally allow us to disconnect from them and go on to build a happier life for ourselves and our families.

The choices our BPD partners make in *their* lives also have consequences in *our* lives. Losing our love may be the price they have to pay for their lack of honesty, humility and courage.

GOD, FOR TODAY, help me to learn everything I can about the disorder which threatens my relationship, my family, my health and my happiness. I trust that the knowledge I gain will strengthen and lead me to the next step I need to take to create the life I deserve.

POT-SHOT NO. 13.

SUDDENLY I LOST ALL CONTROL OF MYSELF, AND STARTED MISSING YOU.

©ASHLEIGH BRILLIANT 1980.

B-O-N-K Medicine

Partner of BPD to therapist: "He hurts me terribly. I'm miserable ... but I *love* him and still want him!"

Therapist: B-O-N-K!! (Sound of large, metal, frying pan hitting the side of client's head.) "If that doesn't work, take two more B-O-N-Ks and call me in the morning."

 GOD, FOR TODAY, help me to keep the pain of my "inner child" under control so I can see my situation clearly. Having possibly chosen my BPD partner to make up for the losses of my childhood, it's sometimes very difficult to have common sense in my *today* moments. Sometimes it seems as if the grieving of my *yesterdays* threatens to drown my *todays*.

Help me to know clearly that no one can abandon me any more, because I've become an adult. I can take care of myself now.

©ASHLEIGH BRILLIANT 1998.   POT-SHOTS NO. 7862.

**WHY AM I
SO OFTEN UNCERTAIN**

**WHAT TO
HOLD ON TO**

**AND WHAT TO
LET GO OF?**

Ashleigh
Brilliant.com
SANTA BARBARA

THE *NO FUN* HOUSE AT THE CARNIVAL

If you've read *Stop Walking on Eggshells* or *I Hate You ... Don't Leave Me* (see Resources and Tools section), you understand the "splitting" (or overvaluation/devaluation) mechanism of the BPD. They use it to protect themselves from pain and feelings of abandonment, real or imagined.

Basically, at the start of the relationship with a BPD, we're put on a pedestal. We're wonderful to them and can do no wrong. Or at least things are good in the relationship at that point.

However, the slightest disagreement, criticism, shade of opinion can be interpreted by the BPD as an all-out assault against their very existence. The previous appraisal is sharply revised –we've hurt them, we're no good, and we're thrown in the trash can.

Whew! It's enough to make our heads spin, not to mention that it cuts our heart to pieces.

In reading Dr. Donald Rinsley's book on the treatment of borderline personality disorder and narcissism (*Developmental Pathogenesis and Treatment of Borderline and Narcissistic Personalities)*, he adds another twist to this whiplashing. Again, if you've done outside reading, you understand *projection* as the BPD not being able to feel their own feelings. They have to say *we* are feeling their feelings in order to give them a reality. They *project* them onto us like an old-time movie projector (imagine your stomach as the movie screen!).

But get this: this is also one of the ways we can be devalued! Dr. Rinsley says BPDs project their feelings onto *us* – and then get hurt and mad at *us* because they think *we* have those feelings. And then they split us! They re-create *us* in *their* minds as *their* persecutor – with *their* projections – and then punish us!!

If you're starting to feel numb inside and your eyes are glassing over, you're in the right spot. When I read this, I felt as if I was in the fun house at the carnival – mirrors everywhere with no reality to be seen – and certainly no fun.

This piece of information underlines even more strongly the need for us to continue to educate ourselves and stay on our toes. If we can at least understand the "why's" of the behavior, it won't hurt so bad, and we can protect ourselves.

Our survival depends on it.

GOD, FOR TODAY, help me to honestly absorb all the information I need in order to take care of myself. Sometimes it feels like I'm walking on red hot coals ... in my bare feet ... blindfolded. I am grateful for all that I've learned so far and trust that "more will be revealed."

POT-SHOTS NO.2630.

WHY DO I KEEP COMING HOME, EVERY TIME I TRY TO TRACE MY TROUBLES TO THEIR SOURCE?

HUMOR

Heard the one about the BPD out on a blind date? After talking for hours about himself, he turns to his date and says, "But enough about me. What do *you* think about me?"

What's the BPD's favorite note in the music scale? "Me ... me ... me ... me!"

(Crass, but it relieves the stress for me.)

 GOD, FOR TODAY, help me to retain and use my sense of humor to successfully finish this chapter of my life.

POT-SHOTS NO. 4126.

©ASHLEIGH BRILLIANT 1987.

I UNDERSTOOD
MOST OF
YOUR MESSAGE,

BUT
WOULD YOU MIND
REPEATING
THE LAST SCREAM?

Ashleigh Brilliant .com

WHERE THE RUBBER MEETS THE ROAD

The more crap you put up with, the more crap you'll get!

The first time I read this, I was stunned. Darn. I wish *I'd* said that. Some people just have a way with words, don't they? After all the eloquence of "setting and enforcing boundaries," "protecting ourselves," "logical consequences" – it really says it all.

How much "crap" are we willing to put up with, anyway? The short (healthy) answer is "none." The long (compassionate) answer is, "Some … as long as it doesn't seriously hurt me or my family, and as long as it decreases and slowly disappears over time."

"Where the rubber meets the road," if we don't give clear messages that we won't tolerate the hurtful behavior *forever*, we'll just get more of the same.

 GOD, FOR TODAY, give me the courage to take the steps I need to take to protect myself from the irrational behavior of my partner. I realize he is ill, but if his ship is going down, I know that I don't have to go down with it.

I am still the most valuable dog, and I *know* how to survive.

© ASHLEIGH BRILLIANT 1981.   POT-SHOTS NO. 2076.

WILL ALL THOSE
WHO FEEL POWERLESS
TO INFLUENCE EVENTS

PLEASE SIGNIFY
BY
MAINTAINING
THEIR USUAL
SILENCE.

Ashleigh Brilliant
.com

POT-SHOTS NO. 4-774.

AT WHAT
STAGE
OF MY
LIFE CYCLE
AM I
SUPPOSED
TO
FIND
HAPPINESS?

Ashleigh Brilliant - com

©ASHLEIGH BRILLIANT 1988.

Gift in an Ugly Package

Alexander Graham Bell once said:

> When one door closes, another opens, but we often look so long and so regretfully upon the closing door that we do not see the one that has opened for us.

When my BPD partner left for the last time, raging at me for all his projections and perceived slights, I thought my world would fall apart, me along with it. I was worn down so far emotionally and physically from the anxiety of never knowing when the rages would hit that his final actions felt like I was pushed off a cliff.

Then I found some NPD (narcissistic personality disorder) and BPD (borderline personality disorder) web sites, and the pieces of my life began to come together. I started on the learning journey that would lead me back through my BPD partner and a BPD mother (my "early training").

After going *back*, my *forward* journey began. I became determined to throw a life preserver to those still swimming in an unknown sea of BPD-ism. I started this book as a survival guide. I began talking one-on-one with other people who were struggling to get out from under their destructive relationships. As someone posted to me on the Internet early in the healing from my pain, "You've been given a beautiful gift in a very ugly package."

What kind of a gift have *you* been given through your relationship with your BPD partner, relative or friend? The phrase that comes to mind is: "Looking for the silver lining."

One of the best tools I've ever learned to relieve depression and snap me out of a *pity pot* is to do a gratitude list. When I finish what always becomes a very *long* list (my health, a roof over my head, a car to drive, food to eat, people who love me, and so on), the sad feelings seem to evaporate as does fog when the sun comes up, slowly disappearing. I begin to see that things aren't as hopeless as I'd been thinking they were.

No matter where we are in our journey, whether the doors are closing or opening (or we're out in the hallway *between* doors), there are things to be grateful for and people we can help.

The knowledge regarding BPD and the tools to cope with it are becoming known. You tell one person, who tells another, who tells another ....

Holding hands, sharing our experience, strength and hope, a circle of changed lives will slowly encompass our world.

GOD, FOR TODAY, help me to step out of my own life long enough to look around and *see* the others who are struggling as I have struggled. I know that each of us can do our part, however small, to carry the message to those who still suffer.

© ASHLEIGH BRILLIANT 1981

POT-SHOTS NO. 2267.

Ashleigh Brilliant .com

HAVING LIVED THROUGH SOME BAD TIMES, I'M LIVING PROOF THAT SOME BAD TIMES CAN BE LIVED THROUGH.

FEELINGS = FACTS = ACTIONS

One of the most confusing symptoms of BPD is that of our partner feeling a *feeling* ("I feel abandoned") ... changing it into a *fact* ("She's abandoning me") ... and interacting with us as if that were really happening, with all their anger, rage and punishment directed at us.

And all *we* did was go to bed for a day, sick with a cold, or we went out of town to care for a sick relative, or we were grieving deeply because someone we loved had died.

This behavior is confusing because it's not tied to the reality that *we* are in. It happens completely inside *their* head, where we can't see it! If we could "see" it beginning to happen, at least we could begin to prepare for it. Then it might not hurt so much.

The SET method in *I Hate You – Don't Leave Me* and the PUVAS in *Stop Walking on Eggshells* (see Resources and Tools) are sometimes helpful here to calm our partner down to a point where maybe we can understand what they're feeling.

When we continue giving them "sympathy or empathy" (SET), they usually react with what's going on inside ... if they're able to put a name to their feeling. Sometimes they'll project the feelings onto us, saying that *we* are the one having the feeling, but as we get more skilled in this area, we'll recognize these as *their* feelings. We can then mirror them back to our partner as *their* feelings.

When they're finally talked down to the point where their emotions are calmer, giving them the "truth" statement puts the two realities (theirs and the real one) side by side. Hopefully, the comparison of the two provides the "reality check" they need to control their overreactions.

If not, this is where the BPD splitting and devaluation happen. It's "off with their heads!" again (our heads, you know).

Living with the uncertainty of the rug being pulled out from under our feet when we least expect it can leave us with a bad case of post traumatic stress disorder and physical and mental health problems.

Continuing to nurture ourselves with education, support groups, friends, and a good-paying job (for economic independence) will protect us from the worst of the stress-related illnesses.

Ultimately, however, if this behavior continues, we have a hard decision to make – would we like to fly on the Hindenburg or take the Titanic? You know the decision … either choice (leave or stay) has its pain.

If our partner is making no efforts to ease the hurt in our relationship, at least the leaving decision has a chance to stop the pain some time in the future.

 GOD, FOR TODAY, give me the strength to stand up to the splitting/ devaluation behavior of my partner. Help me to feel Your presence surrounding me, deflecting the raging words away from me like a shield of armor. My heart is tender and needs protection.

© ASHLEIGH BRILLIANT 1993, SANTA BARBARA.

POT-SHOTS NO. 6197

THINGS ARE SOMETIMES BETTER LEFT AS THEY ARE, BUT YOU CAN'T BE SURE UNTIL YOU CHANGE THEM.

Ashleigh Brilliant.com

Doors that Open and Doors that Close

People of faith seem to go through adversity more gracefully than others, whether it be personal problems or physical health issues. They feel that there's some sort of sense and direction to what's happening to them, even if they can't "see" it yet.

A friend used to tell me how she walked through life:

> Down the hall are all these doors. You knock on the doors, and the door that opens, you go in. The door that stays closed, you're not to go in.

Sounds simple enough ... yet so many times we push ahead with our persistent agenda, sure that with just a little more effort on our part, that door will fly open and birds will sing on the other side.

Not only does the door not fly open, we get our nose bashed when the door slams shut!

My friend also says that before she started living by the above, everything she ever let go of "had claw marks all over it."

 GOD, FOR TODAY, help me to trust that doors are opening and closing for me as is needed for my journey. I know that if the Plan A I thought was happening in my life becomes a closed door, Plan B is already in place. I have only to look for the open door and step through it.

POT-SHOTS NO. 2314.

WHAT IS THIS "REAL LIFE" I KEEP HEARING ABOUT?

© ASHLEIGH BRILLIANT 1981.

AshleighBrilliant.com

POT-SHOTS NO. 4416

PEOPLE WHO NEED TO RECEIVE CARE

ARE USEFUL AND NECESSARY TO PEOPLE WHO NEED TO GIVE IT.

©ASHLEIGH BRILLIANT 1988.

BPD Magnets – Bears to the Honey

In attempting to help a relative recover from a BPD splitting/devaluing breakup of her relationship, I stumbled on a healing truth about the partners of BPDs: We are *very* special people, the finest of the fine.

In their childhoods, most BPDs suffered enormous losses of love and nurturing, self-confidence and self-esteem … and maybe even physical or emotional punishment or abuse. Consequently, their need for love and nurturing is "as deep as the ocean, as wide as the sea."

As a result of their early losses, BPDs search carefully for their partners, cautiously measuring personality qualities and choosing people with whom they feel the most loved – and, more importantly, with whom they feel the most confidence that they won't be *abandoned.*

One of the men in my Co-Dependents Anonymous support group said to me one day, "Lynn, we *look* for women like you."

When I first heard that, the hair on the back of my neck stood up. I felt hunted. Maybe it was the tone of his voice. I felt like prey – vulnerable.

Having walked the full distance now over the red hot coals of a BPD relationship and its ending, I see backwards a little more clearly. *Of course,* they're attracted to us. Our personal backgrounds created enormous capacities for empathy, sympathy, love and forgiveness. We forgive endlessly, and sometimes remain hopelessly optimistic that things will turn out okay – denial, repression, frozen feelings, fear of abandonment and of being alone? Who knows? Whatever it is, we not only are able to give the intensity of love a BPD needs so desperately – it also makes us easy to manipulate.

With so much love to give and our empathic radar on 24/7, it's no wonder we're BPD magnets. They're drawn to us like bears to honey. And if they don't begin to recover, *we* feel like we get eaten alive. In the daily process of living with a BPD, we can sometimes feel so frustrated and beaten down that we forget who we were at the beginning of the relationship.

We're good, kind people. We love quickly and deeply. We usually think the best, no matter what adversity comes our way.

Our BPD partners are careful, discriminating judges of people's characters and personalities. They're *love connoisseurs*.

They chose *us* ... because we're the finest of the fine. We are *gourmet* partners.

 GOD, FOR TODAY, help me to lay down my blaming of myself for being in a painful relationship and the sense of *not being worthy* that I sometimes feel. I know that You love me and that many other people love me also.

I am loved because I have so deeply given love first. The fact that the quality of my love hasn't been returned to me by my BPD partner in the same way I gave it is not my fault.

POT-SHOTS NO.4378.

WHAT YOU OWE TO YOURSELF

CAN BE VERY DIFFICULT TO COLLECT.

©ASHLEIGH BRILLIANT 1988.

BLAMING: A GAME CALLED DODGE BALL

There was a movie a number of years back called *He Said, She Said*, which sounds like the perfect title to the "Blame Game" we sometimes get sucked into with our BPD. We're "damned if we do and damned if we don't" – at least that's the way it feels.

Elyce Benham, the therapist who guides the Land of Oz community board for partners of BPDs (landofoz@yahoogroups.com) once said:

> The blaming stuff is also called *externalization*. It's a way that someone can fend off feelings of guilt and shame by putting the responsibility for things on someone else. It can also be part of *splitting*; i.e., seeing people and things in terms of either black or white.

So what do *we* do? We can see clearly the process *they* are involved in, but how do we protect ourselves?

Keeping silent and avoiding (see the *Moving Target Defense*) only puts off the inevitable. When we're finally cornered, we're hit with a *month's* worth of resentments, instead of just those of today ... and some BPD's have memories like elephants.

Besides that, keeping silent (ducking when they throw the ball at us) is often seen by the BPD as approval of their actions. So we achieve nothing by keeping silent – and they continue throwing the ball at us.

In other words, it looks to them like it's okay to throw the ball at us. Hey, we were dodge ball champs in school, weren't we? Or at least we sure learned how to play that game in our childhood homes – a game played for survival.

A better tactic might be to get ourselves a bat or tennis racquet and just send the ball back where it belongs. We should not accept responsibility for our BPD's feelings or actions. We *do* need to be careful as we hit the ball back to them, though. As we all know, there's a volcano lurking just under their skin.

Validating a BPD's feelings instead of validating the blame is a good way to show our interest in the problem, yet stay detached from it so as not to make it a part of ourselves. Validation helps our BPDs to understand it's okay for them to feel whatever they feel. It just isn't okay to blame *us* for their feelings. We love them, but not *that* much.

Hopefully, over time, this can lead our BPD into gaining a sense of their own responsibility. And a little peace in our lives, thank you very much.

GOD, FOR TODAY, help me to play the *Blame Game* without getting pulled into *dodge ball*. Whether or not my BPD *ever* gets well, the continual blaming erodes my self-esteem and eventually leaves me feeling helpless. I don't want to slip down that far, nor do I deserve it.

Help me find the words to show the love and acceptance I have in my heart for my partner, but also deliver the message that I am *not* responsible for his feelings or actions.

POT-SHOTS NO. 1250.

A TERRIBLE THING
HAS HAPPENED ～

I'VE LOST
MY WILL
TO SUFFER.

Ashleigh
Brilliant · com

© BRILLIANT ENTERPRISES 1977.

Stench With No Name

What *is* it that keeps us so *stuck* in these relationships? For me, it was more than the simple platitude given to me by therapists – that I was *addicted* to my BPD and the relationship.

If I was truly *addicted,* why did I not *unaddict* when I finally learned the name of the disorder my partner had and its symptoms?

The greater truth is that I was caught in a subconscious ritual of behavior I'd learned in my childhood. I placated anger (out of fear), people-pleased (again out of fear), and was easily manipulated by love withdrawal and threats of abandonment (did I mention fear?).

That was the fertile ground upon which the BPD behavior of my partner fell. Together we grew a wonderful weed patch ... until I researched the gardening information on BPD weeds and learned how to turn off the water and fertilizer I was feeding those weeds.

Education regarding BPD-ism was the first thing I needed to *unaddict* myself.

Through all those years of my relationship with my BPD partner, with joint visits to eight different mental health therapists, no one *ever* mentioned BPD-ism to me. The therapists we saw worked on *communication* tools with my partner and me, with *support and strengthening* words for me ... and the misery and fear in our relationship continued.

One family friend with a mental health degree finally had the courage to say *BPD.* I finally had the information I needed. Armed with the right key words, I searched the Internet. I finally discovered the reasons for the pain I'd been living with.

The second thing I needed to get myself unstuck came from the first – education regarding BPD-ism gave me a very *clear* picture of *who* my BPD partner *really* was.

There is such a sense of confusion in a relationship with a BPD, because they're not always the *same person.* We know the good person we fell in love with, but who in the world is this raging beast who appears every once in a while and causes great hurt?

When I first started attending Co-Dependents Anonymous meetings, all I could say was, "I *cannot* get these two people rectified in my mind. I *cannot* get these two people rectified in my mind." (Dr. Jekyll and Mr. Hyde are mentioned frequently on the community web sites for partners of BPDs.)

And then there's the *hoover* behavior. After the BPD has raged at us, and we're walking around with walls of concrete erected around us for protection, they frequently hoover us. (Imagine a giant vacuum cleaner coming down from the sky, sucking us up into it.)

Yep, we get sucked back *into* the relationship (*boomerang loved*) with their overflowing, benevolent actions – flowers, fun things to do, apologies (sometimes), any behavior designed to show us they're *not really who they just showed us they are!!*

It's as if you're in the movie *Gaslight*, where someone tries to convince you that what you see as reality *isn't* reality.

If a sick animal crawls under your house and dies, the odor gets worse and worse. You wander around like a person who's losing their grip, saying, "I *know* I smell that smell, but *where's* it coming from?"

We *know* the BPD disorder is there, because the way they act *clearly* isn't normal. We just can't *see* the disorder, because we don't know its *name*.

With no education regarding the dead animal under our house (the BPD-ism in our relationship), we *can't* find it. Everyone in the house just gets sicker and sicker from the stench.

Dr. David Viscott, one of the first call-in radio psychologists in the United States, used to say, "Stick with the truth ... and the truth will set you free."

The problem with BPD-ism has been *finding* the truth about it.

 GOD, FOR TODAY, I am grateful to be one of those fortunate ones who have the knowledge to set themselves free. I pray for those still in the dark about the stench they can smell but have no name for.

FORGIVENESS

Forgiveness is a frequent topic on the Internet sites for partners of BPDs. Religions and their leaders are quoted, the Nazi/Jewish Holocaust is cited, and our personal recovery is alluded to.

The first reaction to deep hurt and betrayal is usually shock and numbness, then anger, then bargaining and depression. Finally comes acceptance – the five stages of grief.

Some of us hang onto our anger because it's the only way we can give ourselves any sense of power. The splitting/devaluation acted out on us leaves us feeling so very power-*less*.

When we finally get to the acceptance stage – whether it's acceptance of the reality of our situation, the knowledge of the disorder or the ending of our relationship – the surrender almost feels like relief. We give up.

For me, acceptance was a long time coming, due primarily to the many years it took to get the education and knowledge about BPD that I needed.

But what about forgiveness? That's not mentioned in the five stages of grief.

Forgiveness is a voluntary step. At first, all I could do was say, "God, this is too much for me. You take it." I just had to release it and turn it over.

Again, the knowledge about BPD came to my rescue. It became like a sport for me. Whenever I'd feel myself slipping back to old hurts and angers, re-reading about the disorder, its causes and behaviors, would pull me out of it.

I believe we reach pity and then forgiveness for our BPD partners when we truly see the depth of the illness in their disorder – the brokenness, the desperation, the hell hole they live in.

A sense of apathy sets in. The previous energy involved with defending ourselves and trying to figure our partners out dissolves. We fully understand that they have a *disorder*, and only *they* can attempt to heal it. I say *attempt* because it's a deeply injured state that they live in, and it takes a huge resolve on their part to even *begin* the process of recovery. And at this point in time, of those who *attempt* it, only a very small percentage are actually able to achieve what could be considered a *happy* life.

So we release our BPDs. We send them along with as much forgiveness as we can muster at that point in *our* healing. We wish them courage and strength for the lessons that life will be showing them, now that we're not protecting and rescuing them *from* those lessons.

GOD, FOR TODAY, I ask for courage and strength for myself to enable me to walk through whatever stage of grief I'm in. I trust that forgiveness will be a natural step I take sometime in the future – when I'm able.

POT-SHOTS NO. 3323

IN SOME
UNFORTUNATE
CASES,

THE ONLY WAY
TO EXPRESS LOVE

IS SIMPLY
TO LEAVE
THE PERSON
ALONE.

Ashleigh
Brilliant
.com

Orange Juice and Doorknobs

When we want a certain result, we should make sure that result is available in the situation. A friend of mine likes to say, "You can't get orange juice from a doorknob."

That doesn't make the doorknob wrong – it's great for opening and closing doors. Orange juice is available elsewhere.

As we walk along this journey with our BPD partners, they won't be able to meet our needs and desires all the time. Sometimes they may not be able to meet our needs and desires *any* of the time.

Concentrating on themselves and trying to undo the damage of their early years may take all the energy and concentration they have. We sooner or later may have to face the reality that orange juice will never be available from them … they may never get well enough to be a kind, loving partner for us.

What do we do then? We have to learn to give the same level of love and nurture to ourselves that we've been giving to our BPD.

Are we eating well? Sleeping enough? Exercising to get those happy endorphins dancing? How about music to lift our spirits? Fragrances – flowers, candles, bubble baths, perfumes, hot potpourri pots – always make me feel warm inside.

How about hobbies to occupy our minds and stop the obsessing about our problems, his problems, her problems, their problems?

We don't realize we're wearing an emotional hair shirt until we take it off – it feels so good to relax and not scratch all the time.

Loving support and hugs are important also. Good friends to meet with for coffee or actual support groups of people dealing with the same issues we're dealing with are great sources for love and hugs.

And, of course, a good psychotherapist trained to diagnose and treat BPD can be wonderful in helping us understand and cope with the behaviors of our partner. Psychotherapists are a notch above friends. I consider them "professional friends." My friends love me and will listen to me and hold my hand forever. However, the understanding of BPD is slippery and hard to get a firm grasp on. We need *extra* help here. That's where a good psychotherapist comes in.

The bottom line is: We're responsible for taking care of ourselves and our own needs. Whether or not our partner will recover and meet some of those needs in the future is yet to be seen.

What we do know *for sure* is that loving and nurturing ourselves will protect us from the mental and physical problems that plague partners of BPDs.

After all, we're the valuable dogs.

 GOD, FOR TODAY, help me begin just one new activity that feels good to me. Help me to find the courage to say to a friend, "I need a hug today." I am entirely ready to begin gently and lovingly caring for *myself*, whether my BPD partner begins work on his *own* recovery or not.

©ASHLEIGH BRILLIANT 1981.   POT-SHOTS NO. 2307.

I FEEL TIRED,
after my
long journey
through the
past
ten
years.

Ashleigh
Brilliant
.com

Patience for BPDs

Sometimes patience eludes us and we're irritated and frustrated that our BPD partner seems to still be repeating old, hurtful behaviors. Remembering the slogan "Progress, not perfection" can help.

The BPD disorder can't be controlled 100 per cent of the time. Sometimes they *will* lose control. But do they regain it relatively quickly? Do they seek appropriate treatment afterwards?

Our BPDs are learning new skills. They're human, just like the rest of us. I can remember learning how to roller skate – lots of falls and bumps and bruises before I was even a *little* bit competent.

To generate some empathy for our partners, we might attempt to do something differently ourselves. Try something that's simple and very automatic – something we do everyday, probably without thinking about it. Now imagine that for today we'll do that task differently than we've ever done it before.

When I tried this, I kept starting to do it the *old* way. I had to keep telling myself that this time, I was going to do it differently. It must be even more difficult for our BPDs, who are not even sure *how* to do it differently.

Progress, not perfection.

 GOD, FOR TODAY, help me to remember that new ways of thinking and acting take time and energy to learn. Help me to withhold judgment as my BPD partner struggles to retrain himself in more effective life skills. Keeping my eyes trained on myself and what I can do to change *my* character flaws would be a good way to show support to my partner.

POT-SHOTS NO. 3284.

HOW CAN I
WAKE YOU UP,

WITHOUT
SHATTERING
YOUR
DREAMS?

©ASHLEIGH BRILLIANT 1985.

Ashleigh Brilliant
.com

But Who Knew?

I have a good friend whose father is a BPD. Her parents recently celebrated their golden wedding anniversary. Fifty years of hell … with absolutely no knowledge of the *name* of the illness that had infected the marriage, no comfort that it was a disorder (and not her fault), and certainly no guidance as to how to deal with it. Her mother coped with BPD withdrawal, rages, blaming and affairs.

Over those 50 years, her mother read every self-help book she could get her hands on … she prayed … she talked with friends, family and ministers. She and her husband saw many different psychotherapists. *No one* mentioned the N-word (*narcissism,* knowledge of which has been around for the last 20 years) or the B-words (borderline personality disorder).

What they *did* for her mother was try to strengthen her so she wouldn't take the abuse. They hoped she would get the courage to leave her BPD husband. But with three children and no way to support them, what was she to do?

Her faith and spiritual connectedness to God were strong. They carried her through. Finally contracting cancer, she made the crucial step to detach herself emotionally from the painful behaviors. She feared what we hear people say, "He'll be the death of me!"

It's only recently, through my journey and my sharing it with her daughter, that she's found a name for what she's lived with. She's devouring all the information available on the disorder. She's more free with every page she reads.

Conversations with her now consist of going back and recounting story after story of things that happened over the last 50 years. She's able to take her new knowledge and *explain* and understand why things happened the way they did.

We hear, "My husband did _____ (fill in the blank with BPD behavior). He did it because _____ (fill in the blank with knowledge of BPD behavior)."

"But who knew?" she says. Each story always ends with, *"But who knew?"*

With no knowledge of the disorder, she was powerless to do any more than *survive* by her wits, her faith, and her stamina. And survive she did.

But what about us? Thank heaven — *we do know*. At least we know *now*. "But who knew?" fits the backward look into our relationships, but the forward look for us has hope. *We* have the knowledge, and there are now more psychotherapists with the additional training on how to diagnose and treat BPD.

And there are even some psychotherapists who know how to educate and help BPD partners (what a concept!). We just need to find them.

 GOD, FOR TODAY, help me to remember when I'm slipping into depression and pity that things could be much, much worse. I could still be one of the millions of people who don't know the *name of their pain.*

©ASHLEIGH BRILLIANT 1983.   POT- SHOTS NO. 3106.

 I'VE BEEN TRYING DESPERATELY TO SAVE MY MARRIAGE FOR THE LAST 35 YEARS.

Ashleigh Brilliant.com

PERFECT BPD PARTNER

Those who have studied the BPD disorder say that if we're involved with someone who has it, we somehow had *early training* in how to interact with, and respond to, a BPD.

By starting their training when they're very young, elephants are trained to stay tied up to a puny little metal stake in the ground. The young, small elephant doesn't have the strength to pull the metal stake from the ground. When fully grown, the elephant totally believes that the feeble stake still holds it ... so the animal never tries to get free.

How do BPDs *train* the people around them as to how they want to be treated? By either raging at them or withdrawing and punishing them with silence, just to mention a couple of the many and varied ways they train us. These two approaches will frequently happen after something happens to the BPD which results in them feeling hurt, humiliated or abandoned – or they just don't get what they want.

How do *we* respond to their training behaviors?

As children, when we were raged at or ignored in silence, we felt scared, alone and abandoned. We scurried to do whatever we could to get the love of our parent back. And it happened over ... and over ... and over ... for heaven only knows how many years.

As the years went by, we got better at *intuiting* and *anticipating* what would set our BPD parent off. We were well trained now in our actions to people-please, placate, take the blame. We were sad little children with a very unhealthy *learned* way of responding to manipulation now permanently installed in our hardware.

And so the *Dance of Death* of distancing (by the BPD) and clinging (by the BPD partner) is the trap we naturally (subconsciously) fell into with our BPD partners as adults.

Being manipulated by fear was so subtle and done so often on us as children that we weren't even aware of it buried deep in our psyche. It laid there in wait for the *right* relationship to come along, like a ticking time bomb ... or a seed, waiting to be watered.

In the movie *Invasion of the Body Snatchers*, the *bad guys* sucked people's healthy insides out and substituted robots in their place. Our BPDs accomplish something similar when they rage and/or withdraw from us. Our robotic selves automatically respond to that abuse by blaming ourselves and hanging onto the ankles of the abuser.

Where do we go from here? What do we do with the knowledge of how we've been used? What do we do with the anger at our BPD for having shamelessly manipulated us with our own fears?

For me, getting the anger out – expressing it verbally (loud and long) and then writing it down in journals – was crucial to unsticking my fury. Until I had vented that, I couldn't even think clearly. The reality of what had truly happened to me was overwhelming.

Then I began to see that what had happened to me could never have occurred if I hadn't *participated*. Sure, I'd been unknowingly *set up* as a child – but at least *now* I knew.

I understood the 12-Step program saying that, "There are no victims – only volunteers." I think, in defense of us all, I'd like to change that saying to, "There are no victims – only subconsciously pre-programmed volunteers."

Understanding BPD and my unknowing part in our relationship showed clearly that the *stakes* were only flimsy little metal things (temper tantrums and withdrawal into the corner to suck their thumbs). We can handle *that*.

We're all adults now. Knowing how we were *conditioned* as children to respond in fear, we no longer need to be enslaved by it.

We have the power and the strength to pull up the stake and thumb our noses at behavior that used to scare us. We're free now.

 GOD, FOR TODAY, help me to face the reality of how my childhood experiences formed me into the Perfect Partner to the BPD. As my BPD partner works on healing and not using manipulation on me, help me, in turn, learn not to be *manipulatable*.

I know that I can't be abandoned anymore. I am an adult now.

FEELING TRICKED ... AND BETRAYED

In *Narcissism, Denial of the True Self*, author Alexander Lowen states:

> An important element in the seduction process is the nature of the relationship in which it takes place. Seduction is not a marketplace transaction, in which both parties are equal and the rule of *caveat emptor* applies. A shrewd trade is not considered a swindle or a seduction.
>
> Seduction occurs only in relationships in which some degree of trust exists. Swindlers are called con artists because they first gain their victims' *confidence* (emphasis added).
>
> To lead someone astray, (to seduce them), you must first get him or her to trust you. Seduction, therefore, is always a *betrayal.*" emphasis added)

~ ~ ~

And betrayed we feel.

No wonder we feel so tricked when our partner's BPD behaviors first surface. We thought he was a different person. He held his masks firmly in place ("seduced" us) until our hearts were deeply given (confidence and trust).

Admittedly, they didn't do it to *con* us out of something. They need our love as much as we need theirs – maybe more. But *fooled* we were. The Land of Oz website refers to being "hoovered." We're hoovered (suckered?) when we're "seduced" at the beginning of our relationship into believing that they are the person they present to us, masks firmly in place.

Then something happens for those masks to fall. In great pain, we see their true selves. We're hurt and horrified. We stumble along in confusion, trying to figure out where this *stranger* came from.

The "hoovering" happens again, as our partner puts the mask back on again and attempts to control the BPD behavior. We believe once more that the *good* person we see is who they really are. We talk ourselves into believing that the hurtful behavior had a *logical* reason for it. We "hoover" ourselves ....

This happens over and over again – until we are so turned around we can't get our bearings. Somewhere along the line we *finally* learn about the BPD disorder ... and the truth.

Where do we go for comfort when the true sense of betrayal hits? How do we hide when the inescapable feeling of having been played for a fool washes over us? We're like Charlie Brown in the *Peanuts* cartoon – we trusted that she wouldn't do it, but Lucy tricked us with that football again.

We feel like a young, trusting child who offered our most precious possession – our heart – only to have it bruised, beaten, scorned and thrown at the side of the road – road kill with a vengeance. We did nothing to deserve such cruel treatment.

How do we ever recover from such soul-shattering mistreatment and betrayal?

We can start by forgiving ourselves for believing that our BPDs offered us *true love*. That isn't possible when a person has a serious personality disorder. The disorder makes its own rules. The disorder has its own way, even if our partner fights it. Their *love* for us can't change that. But we didn't know that.

We can forgive ourselves for falling in love with them. And if we are still in love with who we *thought* they were, we need to forgive ourselves for that as well.

If we can understand where *we* were coming from when we fell in love with them, and what it was *we* offered them that they couldn't see, then we will be able to love ourselves because of who we are.

We will once again be able to see our strengths and what good people we are. From this starting point, we can begin to start putting ourselves back together again, piece by piece.

We feel like the strawman in the *Wizard of Oz*. The monkeys who fly out of trees have pulled all our insides out, and they're strewn everywhere. Limp and sad, our body sits by the side of the road, trying to figure out how to get our life and our personhood back.

We need re-stuffing ... and re-stuffing takes time.

With good DBT (dialectical behavioral therapy), medication, and *strong* motivation on the part of our BPD, we *may* in the future be given the person we thought we fell in love with.

In the meantime, let's be gentle with ourselves. We are trusting, good people who've been run over by a disguised, punishing, out-of-control M-1 tank.

If we'd known it was coming, we'd certainly have gotten out of its way.

 GOD, FOR TODAY, help me be kind to myself as I look at the reality of my deep feelings of betrayal. Help me to remind myself that I did the best I could with the knowledge I had at the time.

Now that I have the knowledge I've needed all along, I can make better choices.

When I know better, I do better.

POT-SHOTS NO. 2379.

© ASHLEIGH BRILLIANT 1982

Ashleigh Brilliant .com

IN ORDER
FOR ME
TO DO BETTER
NEXT TIME,
ONE THING
IS ESSENTIAL:

TO
SURVIVE
THIS
TIME.

BPD Footprints in the Sand

Not all BPDs are as easily recognizable as others. Many have learned very well over the years how to hide their inner turmoil. I've heard the term *closet BPD* used to describe these clandestine BPDs. I call these people *high-functioning BPDs.*

It can be very difficult to sort out just what in the *heck* is wrong when we're in a relationship with a BPD who is working hard to conceal his true self from us.

Whether male or female, they know that blowing up at us over what seem like small things to us will drive us away from them. They've learned this over the years, as they've lost relationship after relationship due to their behavior. They also know that withdrawing in silence will eventually cause anger and rebellion in us – the opposite of what they want.

SO , they get better and better at hiding the behaviors, keeping their masks on tight, not tipping us off to the turmoil bubbling inside them. Not seeing any obvious behaviors that would tip us off to the simmering, below-the-surface BPD-ism, we go to work for them, become close friends with them, live with them, and even fall in love with and marry them.

Then one day (sometimes the first day of the honeymoon), they drop their mask, and we're in a world of hurt ... and *very* confused.

How can we learn to recognize a BPD from afar? The list of behaviors is long, and not all BPDs exhibit every one of them. In addition, remember they're trying to *hide* them from us until we've given them our heart. (They may be troubled, but they're not stupid.)

I've found it helpful to use what I call the *Quick Test* for a BPD. It has three questions:

a. Does this person rage and punish?
b. Does this person withdraw love and/or attention when they don't get what they want? Or when they feel like you're getting "too close" to them?
c. Does this person have empathy/compassion?

When BPDs don't get what they want or things don't go their way and *we* could do something about it, they'll either rage at us (using blame and projection) or withdraw their love and/or attention from us completely. You know – *the cold shoulder* maintained sometimes for days, weeks, and I've even heard of BPDs doing this for months.

Shame on us for not doing what they want – we deserve the punishment.

Lack of empathy and compassion are sometimes a little harder to detect, but are *core* symptoms of BPD-ism.

My now-deceased mother was a BPD, and I can remember even as a small child hearing her say a critical, sometimes sarcastic, remark to someone. I remember just looking at her and puzzling, "How come she can't *see* that what she said is hurtful to that person? *Why* can't she *see* that?" I knew, even at a young age, that there was something wrong with her. I know now that not only was there lack of empathy and compassion on my mother's part, her remarks were *meant* to hurt and punish. My poor father took the brunt of her anger and cruelty.

Another way to detect lack of empathy and compassion is to apply what I call the *Have a Heart Test*. You know there's an impaired ability to feel empathy for others when you find yourself frequently saying things to this person like, "Lighten up. He's only a small child," or "Have some patience. She didn't mean any harm," or "How can you be so upset at him? He's hard of hearing!"

These three questions of the *Quick Test* frequently reveal *tip of the iceberg* behavior which indicates the possibility of serious pain coming our way from that person if we continue the relationship.

Run – don't walk – to well-trained psychotherapists who are familiar with BPD. They can help us look carefully at the BPD's *footprints in the sand* behavior and decide what kind of a person is really walking with us.

However, do be sure the psychotherapist you choose is *trained* to diagnose a BPD. Since these disorders were only written into the DSM-IV (the diagnostic encyclopedia of mental health professionals) in 1994, most of the therapists currently in practice don't have the training or skills to diagnose, much less treat this disorder ... and they *certainly* don't know how to help the partners of BPDs.

BPDs have serious emotional problems, and we do feel sorry for them. However, *we* have been trained and programmed since early childhood to be manipulated by rage and withdrawal.

So we need protection – from them and from *ourselves!*

We need an *invisible shield* (a *Wacko Protector*, as my friend calls it) to shelter us until we're clear that the new person in our life is safe to trust and give our hearts to – a tool kit in our pocket would be nice, something we whip out like a *Star Wars* light saber the minute we sense danger.

Unless we keep the *Quick Test* questions firmly in our minds as we move through life relating to people, we're almost doomed to continue getting ensnared in the quicksand of BPD-ism over and over again.

As one of my friends says, "I've been married to the same man for 20 years – just different names."

We don't want to do that anymore.

 GOD, FOR TODAY, help me to be aware of the subtle signs that I may possibly be blindly walking into yet another BPD relationship. Help me to *see* what I need to see and *hear* what I need to hear. I don't ever want to hurt that bad again.

©ASHLEIGH BRILLIANT 1985.   POT-SHOTS NO.3484.

WHERE SHOULD I STAND TO GET THE BEST VIEW OF REALITY?

POT-SHOTS NO. G354.

© ASHLEIGH BRILLIANT 1983. SANTA BARBARA.

MY HEAD NEVER LIES TO MY HEART ~

BUT MY HEART SOMETIMES TELLS LITTLE FIBS TO MY HEAD.

Ashleigh Brilliant .com

BPD Resistant At Last

I was listening to a friend in a small town in Colorado talking excitedly about the Federal Emergency Management Agency (FEMA) giving her town a grant of money for *disaster resistance*. They'll use the money to change the way the river runs (so it doesn't flood its banks), start an emergency radio broadcast system, etc.

The term *disaster resistance* started me thinking. I live in California, and we call it *disaster preparedness* here. *Preparedness* implies that I'm going to have to go through the disaster. However, if I *prepare for it*, its effect won't be so bad.

Disaster resistance, however, implies that maybe I don't have to go through the disaster at all — an interesting concept.

Certainly, being in a relationship with a BPD is a colossal *disaster* — emotionally, physically, mentally, psychologically, spiritually and many times financially. Wouldn't it be nice to be *BPD resistant?* — to not be affected by BPD behavior — or even (do we dare even wish) to never again *be* in a relationship with a BPD?

We *can* learn to be BPD-resistant, but it'll take study, time, and practice. It's like exercise — it takes a while to build those muscles. Reading — and re-reading — the section in this book entitled *BPD Footprints in the Sand* is a good start in understanding and being able to see and *perceive* BPD behavior.

The materials in this book in the *Resources and Tools* section are excellent sources of education and emotional healing.

For practice, we can apply the three *Quick Test* questions in the *BPD Footprints in the Sand* section. Using these questions over and over again with our friends and family members will help us begin to carry an internal ruler to measure new people as they come into our lives.

After a while, we'll be able to *sense* a BPD, almost *smell* one. We'll *feel* it in our gut (feels like fear, sometimes).

At this point, we will have created a muscle which will give us *power* in our lives. We'll have control over future BPD disasters.

We'll truly be *BPD-resistant.*

Hallelujah!

GOD, FOR TODAY, I am so very grateful for all I'm learning – about BPD and myself. I am being given the key to mastery over *the pain with no name* in my life. Thank you, thank you, thank you.

BPD Preparedness

With some people, becoming *BPD resistant* is enough (see *BPD Resistant at Last*).

But what do we do about the BPD partners we choose to stay with? Or BPD family members? Some schools of psychotherapy advise walking away from *toxic* parents and relatives, never seeing them again.

These decisions, of course, are for each of us to make. In the past, with no information or tools available to deal with BPD-ism, walking away was sometimes all we could do to get any peace in our lives. But it left us feeling empty, and the pain followed us around for years.

Now we have tools available, with strategies to protect ourselves from the really *deep* pain. Now we actually have methods of interacting with the BPD to help them get in touch with their *own* feelings, and not project them on us – thank you very much! Now we have Internet community boards and lists for online support and advice.

And now we have psychotherapists emerging from colleges and workshops with training regarding BPD. So now we just might have a chance to not only *survive* our BPD relationship, but to turn it around so there's less pain for all involved.

I wrote earlier about *BPD resistance*, or the ability to resist the manipulations and pain of the BPD relationship. In the situation of *remaining* in a BPD relationship, I suggest we consider *BPD preparedness*.

As with *disaster preparedness*, with *BPD preparedness*, we would study all the possible ways *BPD disaster* could strike us – rage, love withdrawal, projection, blame, black and white thinking, splitting and devaluation, jealousy and possessiveness, envy, fear of abandonment, fear of emotional intimacy, etc. And *my* personal favorite – behavior that leaves us feeling like we've been thrown in the trash can.

When we know the ways *our personal* BPD might strike out at us, and we've still decided we want to remain in the relationship, we can plan our responses. Talking this over with a trained therapist – or someone who's at least as aware of BPD behavior as we are – would also be helpful here.

Once we know how we'd like to respond, practicing and rehearsing our responses with another person will increase our success. After all, schools have fire drills, don't they? Why? Because when fear and panic take over, we don't act very effectively. We need to practice and practice so that when the disaster hits, our responses will be automatic – not ones that need to be thought out. When a BPD rage avalanche falls on us, there's no time for *planning*.

There's one aspect in *disaster preparedness* to be aware of, though. Actively planning for BPD behavior sometimes requires resistance and confrontation. Also, if we stop responding to manipulation and anger, if we become unwilling to accept blame from our BPD, we are *changing the script* that our relationship has been based upon.

There's a chance our changed behavior will cause our BPD to escalate their previous behaviors. Some BPDs will end our relationship with them or threaten to do so – all in the name of manipulating us back to our old placating, people-pleasing, fearful behavior.

How we handle this possibility and/or actuality will be as different as all of us are. Some of us will be just as glad they left – we're just relieved and ready to pick up the pieces of our lives and move forward. Others of us aren't ready for that yet. If we fold and go back to old behaviors to save the relationship (for now), we need to go easy on ourselves, to be gentle in our self-judgment. We're not strong enough yet to handle the relationship ending.

These types of relationships aren't over until they're over ... it takes as many times as it takes.

GOD, FOR TODAY, help me to put my fear aside over whether my relationship will end if I *prepare* for BPD behavior. Putting a shield around myself to protect me from further hurt, stress, and physical and emotional illness is my main priority now. I *must* survive this relationship so I can go on to help the others who still don't know the *name of their pain* or how to protect themselves from it.

RULES FOR LIVING WITH A BPD
(OR PARDON US WHILE WE VENT)

Contributed by Randi Kreger, co-author of *Stop Walking on Eggshells* and *Workbook for Stop Walking on Eggshells*:

#1: The BPD is always right. About everything.

#2: If the BPD makes a mistake, see rule #1.

#3: You are a spawn of the devil, unless the BPD wants love right now.

#4: If you don't ask questions about how they are doing, you don't care, you selfish pig. If you DO ask questions, they will snap at you for asking the wrong question, and then complain that you don't ask them any questions.

#5: There is only one way to do everything. The BPD's way.

#6: If you or others have different opinions than the BPD about movies, religion, or any other topic, then those opinions are clearly wrong and even stupid.

#7: The BPD's inner life and feelings are serene and happy, and the fact that they drink, smoke and over-eat themselves to death and have no close friends or real significant other relationships is irrelevant. The BPD needs no one because no one is good enough for the BPD.

#8: If the BPD does have problems, they are caused by someone/everything else.

#9: The BPD never has any problems with anyone besides *you.* So what is wrong with *you?*

#10: You *must* be intimidated by the BPD. If you dare break this unspoken rule, you will be punished, you spawn of the devil.

#11: The BPD reserves his or her abusive behavior for you. Everyone else thinks they're great. You are never, *ever* to let anyone else know what the BPD is really like.

#12: If you say or do something, you will be wrong. If you *don't* say or do anything, or stay away, you will be abandoning.

#13: You are never to let on that you know the BPD's secret; that is, how they really feel inside. If you do, you will be met by screams of denial or worse, you spawn of the devil.

#14: You are a spawn of the devil for even thinking these things, let alone writing them down.

 GOD, FOR TODAY, I want to allow my sense of humor out to play. Living with a BPD can drain me of all laughter and joy. Every once in a while, it just plain feels good to have some fun..

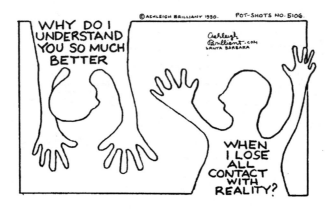

HEROES VS. MARTYRS

"In the spectacle of Death, in the endurance of intolerable pain, and in the irrevocableness of vanished past, there is a sacredness, an overpowering awe, a feeling of the vastness, the depth, the inexhaustible mystery of existence, in which, as by some strange marriage of pain, the sufferer is bound to the world by bonds of sorrow.

"In these moments of insight, we lose all eagerness of temporary desire, all struggling and striving for petty ends, all care for the little trivial things that, to a superficial view, make up the common life of day by day; we see, surrounding the narrow raft illumined by the flickering light of human comradeship, the dark ocean on whose rolling waves we toss for a brief hour; from the great night without, a chill blast breaks in upon our refuge; all the loneliness of humanity amid hostile forces is concentrated upon the individual soul, which must struggle alone, with what courage it can command, against the whole weight of a universe that cares nothing for its hope and fears.

"Victory in struggle with the powers of darkness is the true baptism into the glorious company of heroes, the true initiation into the overmastering beauty of human existence. From that awful encounter of the soul with the outer world, emancipation, wisdom, and charity are born, and with their birth a new life begins."

— Bertrand Russell's *A Free Man's Worship*

I don't believe I've ever seen our journey as partners of BPDs described more eloquently – victory in struggle with the powers of darkness – baptism into the glorious company of heroes – awful encounter of the soul with the outer world.

Before our knowledge of personality disorders, we *were* struggling in darkness. Now we struggle with the "powers of darkness."

Truly, we *are* heroes, as we work to balance supporting our BPD's efforts to recover with *our* need for safety. We haven't abandoned them because they have a personality disorder. We haven't turned tail and run because *their* pain has brought so much turmoil and pain into *our* lives.

But when is enough, enough? By what sign will we know that it's time to throw in the towel? The difficult question for *us* is: At what point do we stop being heroes and turn into martyrs?

GOD, FOR TODAY, show me that I am *not* in "a universe that cares nothing" for my hopes and fears. Besides my spiritual life, bring those people into my life who *do* care about me and support my journey.

Help me to continue measuring and monitoring the progress of my BPD relationship. I want to see clearly when I am becoming a martyr, so I can take action. Remind me that "emancipation, wisdom and charity" and "the birth of a new life" will be my gifts at the end of my struggle with darkness, whether I stay with my BPD partner or not.

MANY PAST WRONGS CAN NEVER BE RIGHTED, ~ BUT MANY FUTURE WRONGS CAN STILL BE PREVENTED.

POT-SHOTS NO. 3299.

Ashleigh Brilliant.com

© ASHLEIGH BRILLIANT 1985.

The Cowardly Lion: Courage vs. Wisdom

The Wizard of Oz to the Cowardly Lion:

> As for you, my friend, you are a victim of disorganized thinking. You are under the unfortunate delusion that simply because you run away from danger, you have no courage. You are confusing courage with wisdom.

Wisdom is something we ask for everyday, as we feel our way through this journey with our BPD partner.

When *is* it *dangerous* enough to run away? *Dangerous* enough to our physical health? Our mental health? Our financial health? Our spiritual health? Our family's health?

In my home of origin, due to the chaos generated by alcoholism and BPD-ism, I had to learn courage far beyond my years. As an adult, I've had friends tell me I'm willing to walk "where angels fear to tread."

Have I not been as "wise" as my friends?

Have I confused courage with wisdom?

I've certainly been more optimistic about outcomes than many of my friends. Co-Dependents Anonymous says some of us "stay in harmful jobs and relationships far too long."

For me, I can only see "far too long" looking backwards. Looking forward is more complicated.

 GOD, FOR TODAY, give me the wisdom to see clearly my life and the direction I'm going. And give me the courage to run away if I need to.

POT-SHOTS NO. 2362.

HERE I AM ~ AGAIN

BACK IN UNCERTAINTY.

© ASHLEIGH BRILLIANT 1981.

Ashleigh
Brilliant .com

THE TIN MAN: AN UNBREAKABLE HEART?

The Wizard of Oz to the Tin Man:

> You want a heart? You don't know how lucky you are not to have one. Hearts will never be practical until they can be made unbreakable. And remember, my sentimental friend, that a heart is not judged by how much you love, but by how much you are loved by others.

An unbreakable heart? Where do we go to get one of those? As we're battered around by blame, projection and splitting/devaluation, it's a nice daydream to think of a heart that couldn't be hurt.

But if our hearts were left unable to be hurt any more, we would have been truly damaged by the BPD in our lives. Healthy hearts aren't walled off and isolated in fear. They're open, trusting, vulnerable – and love pours forth from them.

It's true that we're judged by how much we are loved by others. But wise hearts know they loved first – what we put forth comes back to us – what goes around, comes around – what we sow, we reap.

The hearts of those who choose to stay and help a BPD struggle to recover are large, indeed.

 GOD, FOR TODAY, I want to be aware of my "heart condition." If I'm starting to lose my openness and ability to reach out in love to the world around me, perhaps it's time for a reality check regarding how my BPD relationship is affecting me. Help me to perceive my life without denial or minimizing. Help me to know when it's time to leave.

My "heart health" depends on it.

POT-SHOTS NO. 1279.

SOMETHING
MUST
BE WRONG
IF I GET
HOMESICK
EVEN WHEN
I'M AT HOME.

© BRILLIANT ENTERPRISES 1977.

TEN-COW PEOPLE

Comments by Dr. Sam Vankin written on the narcissism website (www.npd-central.org):

> "… the narcissist affects his victims by infiltrating their psyche, by penetrating their defenses. Like a virus, it establishes a new strain within his/her victims. It echoes through them, it talks through them, it walks through them. It is like the invasion of the body snatchers.
>
> "You should be careful to separate your 'selves' from the narcissist inside you, this alien growth, this spiritual cancer that is the result of living with a narcissist. You should be able to tell apart your real you and the 'you' assigned to you by the narcissist.
>
> "To cope with him/her, the narcissist forces you to 'walk on eggshells' and develop a false self of your own. It is nothing as elaborate as his/her False Self, but it is there, in you, as a result of the trauma and abuse inflicted upon you by the narcissist."

A "false self" (mask) of our own … developed as a result of trauma and abuse from BPD's?

I wrote about this topic from another angle in the *Moving Target Defense*. Walking on eggshells, we understand that. Smiling when we're crying inside, hoping not to set off another round of *zero to psycho* rage – avoiding talking about any topic that might trigger another *nuking* our way.

When our antennae pick up any *possibility* of hurt coming our way, how quickly we can put our *own* masks on. Yet the BPD-caused damage goes into our psyche anyway, doesn't it? Somehow, the words and the intensity of their emotions when we're split and devalued penetrate the walls we try to put up.

A spiritual cancer does indeed begin to grow inside us. The malignancy (malignancies kill, you know) tells us we are what the BPD says we are (even though intellectually, in our heads, we know it's not true).

The growth is small to start with and our intellect easily overpowers it in the beginning. But as shock after shock comes and our self-esteem falls lower and lower – no matter how many times we put on our mask – or how many *different* masks we create to ward off the shocks – we begin to give up.

Our defenses weaken because they aren't *working*, and we have nothing to replace them with. With no knowledge of BPD, we don't know where to go ... or how to help ourselves.

Our real *self* becomes eaten up by the BPD lie instilled in us by splitting and devaluing behaviors and comments. It becomes difficult to separate the truth of who we *are* (or who we *used* to be) from who we're *told* we are.

This reminds me of a study I read once about two groups of dogs who were set on a mat which had been electrified to lightly shock them. The first group of dogs was given a sound signal (bell ringing) just before the shock came. Before long, the dogs learned to jump off the mat when the bell rang and not get shocked.

They had power in their lives and were able to control the pain so it didn't get to them.

The second group of dogs was never given any sound before the shocks came. The dogs had no advance notice and therefore no way to protect themselves. They began to exhibit signs of nervousness and anxiety, pacing up and down, *dog-worrying* about when the shocks would come. Finally, they just gave up and laid down on the mat, resigned to their fate.

Is this how we feel when nothing we do seems to make any difference in stopping *our* pain? No wonder it's so hard to find the strength to leave an abusive relationship when it's continued on for a long time.

The BPD body-snatchers sucked our real self out and left a cringing animal in its place, one who believes all the blaming and projection that's been thrown at it ... one who's been sapped of any strength to crawl away from the pain.

The flip side of this story is who we *could* be if our BPDs were building us *up* instead of tearing us *down*. The reverse of this slow, downward-spiraling malignancy is shown in the Oriental story of the Ten-Cow Woman.

It seems there was a very shy, not very attractive young woman whose family was having difficulty marrying her off (in the *olden times*, ladies!). Getting married at that time meant a man valued a woman enough to present her family with a dowry of valuable gifts.

No man came forth for this woman.

Finally, a man wanted to marry her, and he wanted to pay *ten cows* to the family – a handsome dowry, indeed. Soon after the wedding, he went abroad with his new wife.

Many years later, they returned. The family and villagers were all astonished to see the incredible change in the woman. She stood tall and was very beautiful. She was no longer shy, but beamed with a radiant smile.

When asked what had happened, the husband replied, "I paid ten cows for her and I *treated* her like a Ten-Cow Woman. Over time, she *became* a Ten-Cow Woman."

How different would *we* be if our BPD partners treated us as Ten-Cow People ... instead of as cringing dogs?

 GOD, FOR TODAY, give me the strength to keep my fingers in the dike of my psyche. Help me to shore up my defenses against destructive BPD treatment. Help me to remember who I really am, with all of my good qualities.

I'm doing all that I can to understand this disorder and support my partner as he tries to recover ... but in my heart of hearts, I long to be treated as a Ten-Cow Person. I deserve it.

POT-SHOTS NO. 6776.

©ASHLEIGH BRILLIANT 1975. SANTA BARBARA.

Ashleigh Brilliant .com

WHY DO I SUFFER THE SAME PAINFUL CONSEQUENCES,

EVERY TIME I PERFORM THE SAME FOOLISH ACTS?

Our Mission

I was doing some spiritual reading and chanced upon some old Biblical references to the sacrificing of young lambs.

I've always cringed at the thought of those lambs. They're so small, so sweet and gentle, soft and fuzzy, trusting and open, snuggly and loving, eager to run and play, so unaware in their pure innocence of the dark powers that exist in the world … like an unaware BPD partner.

Ever felt like you were *led to the slaughter??* You made one comment after another, innocently sharing, only to realize with horror that the BPD fires of hell were opening in front of you? And there was nowhere to run!

Each of us as the partner of a BPD is a different person, I know, but I see a common thread of kind, compassionate willingness to love and nurture amongst us all. I suspect these qualities are what drew the BPD to us in the first place. They are in great need of the lamb-like qualities we have to give. And so, in our innocence, we're pulled in, giving the kind of love that makes us feel good inside … only to find ourselves drawn and quartered for some imagined violation.

Gentle lambs shouldn't be punished like that. And in a world where things were fair and just, we wouldn't be in the situation we're in.

So how do we make sense of it all and find a purpose for ourselves in all the confusion and despair?

First, we take care of ourselves – physically, emotionally, financially and spiritually. Then we care for our family in the same way. *Then* we support our BPD in his or her recovery.

However, whether our BPD recovers or not, *we* must survive. There are still millions of gullible, naïve, lamb-like people out there being pulled into BPD relationships every day.

Who will help them, if not us?

We must survive our BPD relationship. Our mission, when we get our *own* lives in order, is to move on to help those who still don't know *the name of their pain.*

There are *so* many others who need our help … they may not make it without us.

GOD, FOR TODAY, help me to know in my heart that my struggles are not without purpose. One day, I will look back and see the beautiful tapestry that has been woven out of my tears and broken dreams. I will be surprisingly grateful for the pain of my past and not want to change it.

It's hard to see right now, but I trust it will happen.

TRYING TO HELP ... JUST ONE MORE TIME

Not knowing *the name of my pain,* I struggled for years trying to figure out where the man I loved would disappear to when he misinterpreted things and raged at me.

When I heard about BPD, I was horrified to learn that the man I loved was a *mask.* He was in there somewhere, but didn't actually seem to reside full-time in his body. The *mask* was merely a front ... not the whole person.

It seems to me that our struggle as BPD partners is that we will always love the *mask.* It's hard to accept the reality of who the BPD really *is* ... that the mask doesn't actually exist.

We're just so sure that if we love them enough, we can make up for what they suffered as children. We mistakenly believe that our love will keep the mask on our BPD, and the person we love will never disappear again. But it's just a mask – the person they're *trying* to be – not the person they really are *behind* the mask.

We want to fill our partner's life with all the love, kindness and support they didn't get as a child ... and so we willingly (although unknowingly) walk to the slaughter of the next hurtful episode.

Often, we will continue for a long time trying to help them. Sometimes, no matter how far we have come in our journey to freedom, no matter how bloody the battle has been, no matter how wounded we are, we will turn around and reach out *one more time* to try to help the BPD in our life – even if we might drown (or lose our life) in the process.

Love does such things. Heads tall, now. To have loved so selflessly is nothing to be ashamed of. Gold star by your name.

However, it's okay to hibernate and lick our wounds when we finally surrender and give up.

If we're halfway up the wall of the pit on our way out of our BPD relationship, it's important not to look down ... or look back. We might be tempted to try to help just one more time ...

 GOD, FOR TODAY, help me to know when it's time to jump from my sinking ship relationship and give me the courage and the strength to do so. I trust that Your life preservers and rescue boats are on the way.

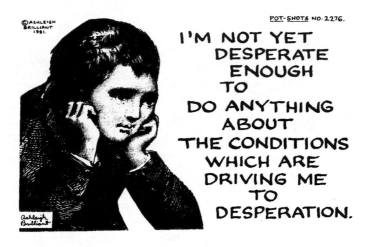

GET OUT OF HELL FREE COUPON

The shame of it all. The incredible searing shame of it all. When the splitting occurs and we're abruptly (with no warning) abandoned or thrown out, or we're publicly raged at, the embarrassment of the Scarlet BPD emblazoned on our chest for all our family and friends to see (again!!) is almost too much to bear.

It doesn't matter that we don't *deserve* it. It doesn't matter that we didn't *cause* it. It doesn't matter that we're struggling just to be able to *breathe* some moments, with the emotional horse's kick in the gut we've received.

And it doesn't matter that we're bright, capable, loving people, either.

What *does* matter is that to everyone looking *into* our lives, all they see is a shambles – a soap opera of emotional drama that makes absolutely no sense at all and leaves *us* looking like fools.

And they're right.

In moments of clarity, we *know* they're right, but finding our way out of the maze is easier said than done. If it were easy, we'd have said good-bye to the painful BPD relationship a long time ago, wouldn't we?

There are moments when we see *clearly* that our partner is *not* getting better, is not doing the work needed to be done, and, in fact, isn't motivated to do anything at all. It's all *our* fault, of course.

We *know* what we should do, so why can't we do it? What keeps us tied to them? Why do we endure one splitting episode after another, picking up the pieces, making excuses for the BPD behavior, and patching our lives back together one more time?

We need a *Get Out of Hell Free* coupon ....

Besides knowing our BPD partner is sick ("in sickness and in health," you know), children to care for, economic fear (isn't that enough?), there's yet another invisible chain that may be the core reason we stay *stuck*.

Patrick Carnes, Ph. D., has written a book called *Betrayal Bond: Breaking Free of Exploitive Relationships*. In it, he says the trauma experts and the addiction experts were seeing similar behavior but not combining their knowledge into information that could help people change their lives.

The trauma experts were seeing people with serious post traumatic stress disorder after painful childhoods and adult relationships. The addiction experts were seeing people in what they called *addictive relationships* – people unable to break away from painful situations – love relationships, jobs, family members.

Carnes says that when the right chemistry of loving care is created, alternated with fear, terror, threats, degrading behavior or violence, a *trauma bond* is formed.

We've all bonded to our BPD partners with what was initially an affectional *love bond*. As the nonsensical, out-of-the-blue, in-your-face blaming, projection and rage flew at us, we became trauma bonded to them.

This is a very insidious, powerful web to break out of. It's a form of brainwashing. Heard of the *good kidnapper – bad kidnapper* routine? The bad kidnapper roughs the person up emotionally (fear is used). Then the good kidnapper comes in and is kind and sympathetic. They use it to *break* people – tear them down emotionally. It weakens them progressively so they finally give up.

I believe this was the conditioning I received in my childhood home from my BPD mother. (Remember the baby elephant tied to the stake.)

Combining fear with kindness is such a powerful tool to cripple a person psychologically that the military trains its personnel in how to resist it (where do we sign up for that course?).

It's a psychological warfare tool used in concentration and prisoner-of-war camps … and here I thought I was in a marriage!

Carnes explains that trauma bonds can be formed almost instantaneously (one raging/splitting episode would do it, wouldn't it?). And even though they can be *formed* almost instantaneously, they can last *forever*, sucking us deeper and deeper into a trauma bond that we can't get out of.

Forever gives our BPD partner *lots* of time to continue breaking us down. Sadly, an image of an abused dog slinking along the walls comes to mind … no wonder our bodies begin to break down and get sick.

Carnes' book is a workbook to discover childhood trauma bonds, create awareness of current trauma bonds, and begin a path of action to lead us out of the maze. I heartily recommend it for those who need a ride out of hell.

 GOD, FOR TODAY, help me to open my mind to yet another *theory* regarding why my life is in such chaos. I've read so much and tried so hard … sometimes it just seems hopeless.

One thing I *do* know, though: I *deserve* a happy and joyous life. If my BPD partner isn't going to do *his* part, it's entirely up to me. I may be digging out with a spoon, but eventually, I *will* get out.

GET OUT OF HELL FREE COUPON

You gave it your best shot.

It was a game you couldn't win.

Game over.

Move on.

**HOW DARE YOU
GET ALONG
WITHOUT ME!**

POT-SHOTS NO. 2126.

Ashleigh Brilliant .com

IF YOU HIDE YOUR REAL FEELINGS FOR LONG ENOUGH, YOU MAY EVENTUALLY FORGET WHAT THEY ARE.

© ASHLEIGH BRILLIANT 1981.

BPD Awakenings

Then there's the issue of medication for our BPD. Anyone been down *that* rocky road?

Many mental health professionals have had good success with motivated BPDs who will submit to medication to calm their over-reactiveness, followed by long term cognitive therapy.

Medication was one of the last straws I clutched at before my BPD's final splitting/devaluation rage engulfed me.

And it was wonderful. They say the medications can take up to six weeks for a person to notice a change. My partner was a different person the second day. This is called a *good responder* (no kidding!).

Being good responders means their brain chemistry was starving for the chemicals. That's why so many BPDs are alcoholics or drug addicts or overeaters. Early in life, they found chemicals that made them feel better ... but they were addictive.

On medication, my partner wasn't irritable anymore. He laughed out loud over small things. He didn't take offense at statements I made. He was interested in planning social get-togethers with me.

He became a happy man.

I started dropping my automatic flinch that I had developed when I spoke to him. ("Will he be angry at what I'm about to say?") I began to walk flat-footed (off my tiptoes). I could feel the tenseness in my body start to relax.

I stopped holding my breath ... I could finally exhale.

It was five months of bliss. I tried to mirror back to him the value of the medication by asking if he noticed the difference in *me* – how relaxed and responsive I was to him. He had noticed.

I asked about his work. He said people were coming up to him and asking what had happened to him. He seemed so much happier and content.

We should have ridden off into the sunset on white horses ... to *live happily ever after.*

It didn't happen that way. He began to say he felt "too happy" (Too happy? Who wouldn't want to be *more* happy?) He started taking *medication holidays*, as he called it (skipping days here, days there, in taking his medication).

And suddenly, the rages were back – seemingly worse than before. Maybe cold turkey from the medication can cause this … I don't know.

I became like a deer in the headlights – frozen. I had dropped my protective walls so completely (obviously a mistake, in hindsight) that I had no protection and nowhere to go.

And then the grief set in. I felt like I'd been in the movie *Awakenings*. The people in the movie were in a mental hospital. They were given a new medication which brought them out of a hellish non-existence into a flourishing, happy life. But the medication didn't last, and slowly each of them slid backwards to their former, mentally imprisoned selves.

I had touched my partner's happiness. I had seen with my own eyes the actuality of him living day after day with a smile on his face and a lilt in his walk. That which I had hoped and prayed for for so many years had happened … the man I loved was back.

But it was taken from me – and from him – and I had no power to change it. Sorrow doesn't even begin to describe the emotion. That deafening sound you hear is all my hopes and dreams crashing down … one more time … this time to fall even farther, because I knew it didn't have to happen.

Why in the world would someone stop taking a medication which made them feel so good? Because there was no therapy to back it up and hold it in place.

The cognitive distortions of a BPD (*stinking thinking* as Alcoholics Anonymous calls it) will eventually undermine and destroy any forward movement. The misconceptions of the BPD regarding what's actually happening around them cause them to believe *they* have no problems. They believe it is *us* and *our actions* that are causing all the difficulties. Extending this thinking out logically, they then decide there's no reason for *them* to take medication for something we are causing. That's why AA calls it a disease – "cunning and baffling."

So if you'll pardon a little advice from a war-torn victim: Be careful not to let your family general practitioner prescribe an antidepressant (or any mental health medication, for that matter) for your BPD without a fully-trained psychotherapist being part of your team. This is necessary for your partner and for *you*.

If your partner won't go for therapy, by all means, you must go. The therapist can look down the road and help prepare you for what's coming next.

In the future, the treatment for BPD will become well-known and established. People won't have to work so hard to get help. But right now, we're still in the *early pioneer* stage of this disorder. Getting the right treatment sometimes seems like panning for gold – we need lots of hard work and a healthy dose of good luck to boot.

Circle your wagons, good friends. Share your knowledge, support each other, and choose the pathway of your journey *carefully*.

Without good knowledge of BPD and a trained psychotherapist to guide us, we often choose the wrong road. As pioneers, we don't want to end up like the Donner Party.

 GOD, FOR TODAY, help me to find the medical and mental health professionals who truly understand the nature of this disorder which imprisons me and my family. I long for love, laughter and happiness. I'll pull my covered wagons along whatever path I'm shown, to find the peace I so desire.

TOMORROW IS ANOTHER DAY ~

BUT I HOPE IT'S NOT ANOTHER DAY LIKE THIS ONE.

POT-SHOTS NO. 2976.

Ashleigh Brilliant
.com

© ASHLEIGH BRILLIANT 1983.

ALLOW ME
TO CONGRATULATE YOU
ON THE SKILL
WITH WHICH
YOU HIDE
YOUR
DEFECTS.

In Defense of Ourselves

"Well, you must have known what he was like before you married him!" How many times have we heard *that?* Or seen it on the faces of our friends, families – even therapists?

What they don't understand is that the person we made the commitment to is *not* the person we eventually ended up with.

Most BPDs bring out their behaviors very slowly. They emerge gradually, over time. During that process, we become so conditioned to the behaviors that they seem *normal* to us. And so we learn to accept the unacceptable.

In addition, since the BPD is usually so self-focused and/or causes so much chaos in our lives, we as partners slowly lose connection with our support systems of friends and family. We have no feedback as to what *is* normal – what's acceptable behavior and what's not.

Pretty soon we're ripe for brainwashing. We question our perceptions and are powerfully drawn into the belief that *we* are at fault for nearly everything.

Who falls in love with a person who presents themselves like that right from the start? And who would *stay* with a person who behaved like that right from the start?

People forget that by the time the FOG clears (fear, obligation and guilt) well enough for us to see the truth about BPD, we've been in the relationship for a long time. Now we have financial obligations, children, family connectedness, businesses started together – and yes, trauma bonding.

Getting out isn't as easy as it looks to someone on the outside looking in.

GOD, FOR TODAY, help me to hold my head high and not feel ashamed of how my life has become such an embarrassing experience. At least now I know the truth and the *name of my pain.* I can now begin putting the pieces of my life back together again … with or without my BPD partner. But I *will* get my life back.

WILL WE EVER *REALLY* BE SAFE?

Narcissistic personality disorder … borderline personality disorder … will our partners ever really be *cured* … *healed*? Will our lives ever be *normal*? Or even *close* to normal? Will we ever live a life with no fear in it?

Sometimes I wonder …

The mental health professionals say adamantly that these personality disorders cannot be *cured*. They use descriptive words such as *maladaptive, chronic, pervasive, enduring* – scary words when they're referring to our partner.

Mental health professionals also say that the personality disorders can only be *"moderated, controlled, modified, lessened"* – by the BPD, not their partner.

And, the BPD must be *strongly* motivated to want to change the behaviors for the above to happen.

I was in a 12-Step group meeting where this message came through loud and clear. The person sharing was talking about fighting his obsession with leaving his spouse … again. He had left her many times, each time blowing up and blaming her for all sorts of things.

They call this *cut and run* behavior in 12-Step programs. Feel the hurt (real or imagined) and run away, lobbing blame and projection grenades over the shoulder. With the education we now have regarding BPD behavior, we can see that this person sharing in the 12-Step meeting was attempting (in fighting his obsession) to control his splitting/devaluation process.

My feelings were of deep sadness for this person's spouse. Besides identifying with her (hey, I've had those grenades thrown at me!), I knew what kind of person she was. I knew her to be kind and especially trusting. She was sitting at home at that very moment, trusting that her partner was at a meeting and getting better every day … and he's talking about abandoning her.

He managed not to be impulsive, to control his *stinking thinking* (again, 12-Step talk) and to put off the leaving for a while. A few weeks later, the urge was gone. He was smiling again. His wife must have done something (unknowingly) that allowed her to be split good again and placed back on the overvaluation pedestal. Little does she know how shaky that pedestal is.

I wonder if she – and all of us in relationships with BPDs – need to realistically accept that we will always live under the knife – just a few steps away from traumatic pain over which we have no control.

All control is really in the hands of the BPD partner. Try as we might, we can't see inside their heads to know what's *really* going on there, to protect ourselves in advance of their actions.

I wonder if we'll ever *really* be safe …I wonder ….

 GOD, FOR TODAY, help me to do what I can to protect myself and my family – emotionally, physically and financially. I'm struggling to reach a balance between being supportive of my partner while also creating a safe environment for us.

I'm sometimes not sure it's possible, but I'm trying.

Aftermath Recovery

I had lunch with a friend recently who had ended a BPD relationship many years ago. Even though she has survived emotionally, physically and financially, I couldn't help but notice the deep woundedness she still carries with her.

The aftermath ... when it's over (whether we leave or whether our BPD begins to heal), is still the same.

There's a sense of having been violated – a basic feeling of personal betrayal at a very deep, soul level. And it never goes away completely.

Even though we reach a point of *understanding* the disorder – maybe even a true *forgiveness* for the pain we've received – it's as if a basic innocence has been lost in us.

We're aware now that the true personalities of people can be hidden. We now know that some people are literally walking time bombs, with invisible booby-trapped wires hanging off them, just waiting for a sensitive touch from others to explode.

We sometimes end up after one of these relationships with our own form of intimacy fear – like a disease we caught from our BPD partner.

My friend has chosen to wall off, due to intimacy fear. Emotionally, she's just distant from people. She doesn't invest a lot of herself in relationships. That way, she can't be hurt ... but I think she must be lonely and sad inside that wall.

She's paid a high price for loving and trying to help a sick person.

I have another friend who lived her entire married life with her BPD partner, never knowing *the name of her pain.* To protect herself, she walled off physically and emotionally *within* the relationship. In the process, she lost touch with who she was. Sometimes we hide ourselves so well we forget where we put ourselves.

Now that this second friend has been emotionally freed by knowledge of BPD, she's slowly picking up the pieces of who she used to be and putting herself back together again.

The story of the Straw Man in the *Wizard of Oz* movie fits here. I can just see that Straw Man, sitting in the middle of the Yellow Brick Road with all his insides scattered around him (after the monkeys that fly out of trees attacked him). He picks up handfuls of straw and stuffs them inside his shirt, putting himself back together again, bit by bit.

Where has *your* straw been scattered? Who did you *used to be*? What did you like to do before your downward emotional slide began?

Sometimes, before we can start doing things we used to like to do, we have to do even more basic work … such as therapeutic activities to heal our insides.

I started singing in my church choir. I can't sing very well, but most church choirs aren't highly selective. I wanted a church *family* around me, but was pleasantly surprised at the additional gift of spiritual melodies sailing around in my head all week long.

And laughter. Life had been such a struggle and so gosh-darned *serious* for so long … I just plain needed to laugh again. So I rented funny movies, read joke books, and finally joined an improvisational comedy group. Once a week, I would go to their workshops and just laugh and laugh at their antics. My heart was crying inside, but I forced myself to go. The laughter began to heal me from the inside out.

What do *you* need to do to start healing? Walk on the beach? Music? Art? Dancing? Whatever it is, find a way to start doing it … today.

If we don't start our *own* healing, the BPD disorder will have claimed *two* people instead of one.

 GOD, FOR TODAY, give me the strength to just do one thing for myself that warms my heart and nurtures my soul. I want to turn around the downslide I'm in and make it an *upslide*.

The Incredible Walking Door Mat

The Big Book of Co-Dependents Anonymous states:

> Codependents compromise their values and integrity to avoid ejection and other people's anger; codependents are extremely loyal, Remaining in harmful situations too long.

I remember the first time I truly, clearly, deeply felt it. To the absolute core of my being, it felt like abject *terror* – the fear of a cornered, small, defenseless animal with nowhere to run, waves of fear washing over me to the point of nausea ... so very, very terrified. I had felt the fear before, in a vague sort of way, but had never felt it to the point where I actually gave it a name.

It happened the fourth time my BPD partner raged at me and slammed his way out the door. I had been worn down emotionally over a long period of time, not knowing that I was being manipulated by unconscious internal emotions that needed to be beaten back, no matter the cost.

For me, the process had been working something like this: someone I loved would hurt me, and a deep, almost primal fear would take me over. As I look back now, it was so deep that it almost resembled what some people describe as a *panic attack*.

This fear feeling was one of absolute, sheer terror that might be felt by a little, cringing child, totally powerless to take care of itself or fend off the frightening abuse coming toward it. And, although I wasn't conscious of it, that terrified feeling *had* to be dealt with and soothed, even at the cost of my own well-being and dignity.

My attempts to feel *safe* when this unconscious terror came over me took many forms. I've written about them in earlier parts of this book – the plastic smile on my face, the walking on eggshells (waiting for the shoe to drop), the dodge ball defense, the ankle-clinging, do-anything-to-please-you person I've been so many times in the past.

Such a sweet, manipulatable person I was, desperate for love and driven by fears of which I had no conscious knowledge. I feel sorry for her now. She just didn't have enough strength to fight for herself, not to mention the fear of not having enough money to care for her children (if she ever *got* the strength to confront those who were hurting her). She was a terrified three-year-old in those moments, doing the best she could with what she had.

The turning point came as an epiphany, when I first consciously *felt* the deep, searing terror. It was an overwhelming moment. I really hadn't *perceived* its existence as a reality and driving force in my life before that point. I'd just been falling from one scared moment to another, trying to flee from all of the terror feelings and make them go away with people-pleasing behaviors. And, of course, as we all know, all that did was encourage the hurtful behavior even more.

The Co-Dependents Anonymous support group states that behavior based on fear of abandonment will *sabotage* our lives. Sabotage! Big word meaning to take a life that was meant to flourish, live in freedom, love others and be loved, achieve good things in the world – and totally derail it, push it to the side of the road, wheels spinning, going nowhere, rendered powerless and beaten.

How do we become free from sabotaging our own lives? How do we walk away from hurtful behavior from lovers, family members, even our employers? More importantly, how do we *stay* away from them and keep ourselves from running back into the relationship when terror and the fear of being alone hit us full force?

The first step for me was to isolate – and name – the feeling. At last I knew the enemy – the demon that was driving my behavior and destroying my life. After that, my head was in charge.

I've heard the saying that we go into relationships with our head and our heart. My head knew the enemy, and my terrified heart absolutely had to be comforted … and ultimately overcome.

Now, overcoming a terrified heart isn't an easy task. In the beginning, going to Co-Dependents Anonymous meetings – as many a week as I could fit in – kept me from drowning. As my faith in a force greater than myself (for me, this was God) became stronger, as He acted in my life to care for me (new friends, new jobs, wonderful new opportunities), I began to not feel so alone. Even in a room by myself, I felt loved and protected. I could finally say, "No," to a relationship where someone was hurting me, and walk away.

Now that does not mean I don't wage a huge internal battle with myself at those times – head struggling with my terrified heart that wants so badly to give that hurting person one excuse after another for how they act toward me. They call it *self-hoovering* on the Land of Oz website. It also doesn't mean that I don't sometimes just cry like a baby, re-feeling those lonely, scared child feelings all over again.

What it *does* mean is that I don't *give in* to those demon feelings. Somehow, someway, I crawl out at the end, having beaten my terrors back, and still am able to turn to the hurting person and say, "Ouch! That hurts." Simple message, simple delivery.

I'm an adult now, even though that small, cowering, terrified child and her feelings still reside deep within me. I know my *head* is strong enough now to out-wrestle my fearful heart and make healthy choices as to who I will *allow* in my life – and who I will *not*. Even though I may love them (and they love me, in their true, inner hearts), I *refuse* to allow their present-day behavior to hurt me. I deserve better.

I know now that whenever hurtful interaction happens, I must reverse my previous sabotaging behavior, stand up for myself, and stop being the Incredible Walking Door Mat.

 GOD, FOR TODAY, help me to feel Your presence in my life. Soothe me as I attempt to quell my fears and make healthy choices for myself. Give me courage as I take my first baby steps in learning to stand up for myself. Help my head to overcome my demon fears and my overly forgiving heart.

POT-SHOTS NO. 2.322.

WOULD YOU CARE TO VIEW THE RUINS OF MY GOOD INTENTIONS?

© ASHLEIGH BRILLIANT 1981.

Identity: Who Am I?

In my childhood, I had to think quickly, assess the mood level of my alcoholic mother, and adjust accordingly. If she was sullen and moody, I moved *carefully*, walking on eggshells at a tender age. If she was angry and rageful, I tried to make myself invisible – *disappear* myself.

If my mother was relatively calm, I relaxed – but ever on the alert to detect possibilities of criticism, sarcasm and mood change, ever ready for the internal, fearful cry of, "Incoming! Incoming!"

I became quite skilled at altering *Who I Was* to survive. This became my identity and my survival mode in my home.

Outside the home, I worked hard, reaching, grasping for praise and admiration. In actuality, the praise and admiration were cheap love substitutes, but they helped me survive.

In high school as a graduating senior, I had high grades in honors classes, was the top dog in the Flag Corp (twirling not one but two flags, while blowing a whistle and leading a group at the same time!), editor-in-chief of the monthly school newspaper, won contests in speech and foreign language tournaments, on and on. I loved it, but that component of needing other people's praise to compensate for the many things lacking in my home was still there.

Professionals call this *overachievement* or *workaholism*. Even today, as far down the recovery road as I've come, I still have to watch this behavior. My first instinct when pain hits is to *get busy* ... put on a smile and run from the pain, rather than stay and deal with it. It was a healthy move in the short run (rather than drink or take drugs), but devastating in the long run. This behavior sabotages my life. Overworking doesn't make the hurtful behavior go away – I continue to be hurt, and things go downhill from there.

I know now that emotional pain is an indicator that something is wrong in my life – that something needs attention, not denial, not running away from it. Forcing myself to stop and figure out *where* the pain is coming from allows me to decide what *action* needs to be taken to *stop* the pain.

"I have a headache. I'll take an aspirin."

"He's hurting me. I'll confront him about it and leave him if he continues."

"My head hurts. I'll stop banging it against the wall!"

But how do we know our *pain* is being caused by a disorder with an actual name, symptoms, and a mental health diagnosis? Not knowing we're dealing with a personality disorder, we struggle onward, showing a false smiley face to the world, *busy* forever in activities that help us feel loved (if only for a few minutes) ... but inside, we're puzzled, confused, hurting.

In my senior year of high school – that far back – I had a deep awareness of this falseness, the fake identity (mask) I wore for the world – the brave little tin soldier who marched alone inside, grieving, ashamed, lonely, depressed.

I tearfully wrote a poem late one night. It talked about feeling like a clown with two faces – the happy, jolly (pretend) one for the world – and the one in tears inside. I suppose that must be the universal human appeal of clowns – little tears painted on their cheeks as they run around in bright, silly costumes that deny the pain in their hearts.

I'm only now beginning to see that our journey here is to discover and know Who We Are, truly. And relationships are the key to this journey, but in the middle of this BPD process, we lose ourselves – our true identity.

Relationships – good or bad – are opportunities to truly *know* and *experience* Who We Are.

How can we know how loving we are if no one needs our love? How can we know how honest we are if no one gives us the opportunity to cheat? How can we know how strong we are if no one tries to overpower us? And how can we know we're good people if others don't do mean, seemingly cruel things to us?

If I'm in a relationship with someone who loves and supports me, I absolutely flower. I'm not afraid to reveal the *inner me* – my thoughts, feelings, wishes, desires, goals, dreams, fears, loves.

And in such sharing, I touch and act upon the true core of Who I Am – what I'm truly *about* here on this planet, the journey I want to make, what I want to accomplish, what I want to change, and what I want to contribute. It's exhilarating!

But what of the deep, searing pain of a BPD relationship? How can I *know* and *experience* Who I Am *there?*

In the deepest of my pain, I have learned the depths of my compassion for others in pain. In having to dig within myself to find the courage to confront the abusive BPD behavior and leave it, I learned how strong I really am. No one will ever walk on me this way again. Nor will I allow anyone else to do this to another in my presence, *especially* to children.

In my struggle to understand what in the world was wrong with my BPD partner, I saw my infinite ability to love and forgive – a precious possession, indeed. In my plodding, grueling, *I will not give up* journey of looking under every rock to discover *the name of my pain* (BPD-ism), I saw my tenacity in the face of adversity, my *absolute unwillingness* to give up until I have the answer I'm looking for.

So now, looking backward, I can see what wonderful experiences my painful relationships have been … at least now that they're finished!

It's all been about discovering *identity* – Who I Am.

All of my relationships have been opportunities to demonstrate Who I Am to myself. I had depths within myself that I didn't know were possible.

Now that I clearly know Who I Am, the next half of my life will be such a thrill. I can hardly wait to see the directions I'll take, the new people who'll come into my life, the places I'll go, the things I'll accomplish.

What about you? Who Are You? Where are *you* in the *identity journey?*

Are you still *struggling with the darkness* to figure out Who You Are? Then keep on! Somewhere down the road you'll discover that you're someone who is no longer willing to be hurt by someone else. You'll know to the core of your being that you're someone worthy of love that doesn't leave or punish … and you'll start dreaming of how to get that kind of love in your life.

Dreaming is the first step to obtaining.

Are you still feeling the pain and depression from the craziness you've been living in, the overwhelming feeling of powerlessness in

your inability to change the behavior of your BPD? Stay with the feelings and let them wash over you. At the end of that deep intensity,
you'll find your backbone of steel that says, "I won't be treated this
way any longer – nor will I allow my children to be treated this way or
raised in this environment."

Onward, brave little tin soldier. The world awaits you with open
arms. Such a celebration is planned for your homecoming.

 GOD, FOR TODAY, help me remember to be
gentle with myself as I make this journey. I know
what I'm working on now. Learning Who I Am
as a loving human being in Your world is a lifetime goal.

© BRILLIANT ENTERPRISES 1971   POT-SHOTS NO. 293

I'M IN SEARCH
OF MYSELF —

HAVE YOU SEEN ME ANYWHERE?

© BRILLIANT ENTERPRISES 1971   POT-SHOTS NO. 278

DUE TO CIRCUMSTANCES
BEYOND MY CONTROL,
I AM MASTER OF MY FATE
AND CAPTAIN OF MY SOUL.

Ashleigh Brilliant.com

POTPOURRI – REALITY TICKLERS

- Last words from a BPD in a divorce – "I'm *not* a BPD!! You just didn't give me enough attention!!"

- Eventually you come to realize that there was *no* reason to consider the feelings of someone who just *hurt* you continually.

- It's very easy to confuse compassion with co-dependency.

- Co-dependency issues are self-denial issues – "You can do anything to me as long as you love me."

- Some really smart people grow up and just *live in their heads*. It's easier not to feel pain that way ….

- If my BPD was doing *physical* harm, the abuse would be obvious. But if we're *emotionally* abused, then first we have to explain it to them and why it's wrong. There is something insidious about being hurt and having to explain *why* we hurt, because someone else's view of reality is so distorted.

- Ultimatums are not obligations.

- Personality disorders are like one-armed bandits in a casino. We keep putting money in, expecting a pay-out. The machine flashes its lights, states the current jackpot and generally looks like a payment is coming. We may get small payments, but we never get the jackpot. The purpose of the flashing lights and small payouts is to ensure that we keep putting our coins in.

- In my relationship with my BPD, I felt like I'd been torn apart, piece by piece, as if I'd been kidnapped from life. I can feel again now – and laugh.

- The anger and rage that is so absolutely justifiable – and has to be *felt* when your life has been ravaged by a BPD – also has to find an end.

- BPDs can often be bright and intelligent and appear warm, friendly and competent. Sometimes they can maintain this appearance for years, until their defense structure crumbles. This usually happens around a stressful situation, such as the break-up of a romantic relationship, death of a parent, or serious illness.

- Comedy and real humor are not about hurting but about saving. Humor is the refuge of the powerless. The jokes about BPD reflect the powerlessness some of us feel in the face of that condition and the deep, deep sorrow.

- BPD relationships are *intense* but stormy and unstable. The intensity of what I *thought* was love in the relationship was what kept me yearning for so long in my healing process.

- Our task: To attend fully to how things *are* in the present moment – and not to how things *could be* or *once were*.

- B-I-T-C-H: Babe In Total Control of Herself

- Give your energy to a BPD and you give it away.

- Leaving a BPD relationship: nominee for the *Cold Turkey* poster kid award

- Jumping through hoops to keep the BPD from withdrawing – or to bring them out of withdrawal: the *devotion test* to *prove* our love for them

- Forgiveness is needed, but forgetting isn't. Otherwise, how would we ever learn? The past can be an omen of what is to come, unless true change is the focus.

- I'm pretty much the same *giver* that I always was. I'm not nearly as good being with a *taker* as I used to be, though.

- Dreams and nightmares must be fed to be kept alive.

- It takes a turning point to free oneself from hate, prejudice and love.

- If you are co-dependent on a desert island where there is no one there to take advantage of you, are you still co-dependent?

- He was like this before I met him, he was like this during our time together, and he'll be like this *long* after I'm gone. It has *nothing* to do with me.

- If it doesn't come out in the wash, it'll come out in the rinse.

- The abuse situation with a BPD is hard to see (compared to physical abuse) because of the gaslighting, constant rearranging of facts, and the cyclical nature of the *I love you so much* statements.

- To forgive or not to forgive – the key is education and understanding. Once we understand how deeply injured the BPD is, the scars from the hurt begin to fade ... replaced with something that feels like pity.

- BPDs are all actors, and we are the stage they walk on.

- Pathological BPD-ism leads to dependence rather than to interdependence, to conflict rather than to collaboration, to sadistic behaviors rather than to tender emotions. It is a malignant form of BPD-ism, because it takes over the host and then kills it.

- A pattern of impulsive flight or *retribution* (punishment) exists in situations where the BPD feels anxious and can't cope.

- Don't be an *N-abler.*

- Mark Twain on singing pigs: "Never try to teach a pig to sing. It's a waste of time, and it annoys the pig."

- Once you accept an idea, it's an idea whose time has come.

- New American Standard Bible, Matthew 7:6: " ... do not throw your pearls before swine, lest they trample them under their feet, and turn and tear you to pieces."

- BPD-ism: the counterfeit human

- An BPD evidences resistance to the *control* of someone else's love for them – they feel controlled when someone loves them!

- The BPD frequently cannot and will not change. They truly, deep down, do not, and never will, believe there is anything wrong with them.

- If you do not know what direction to take, you have not acknowledged where you are.

- Become an *uncooperative* doormat – someone unwilling to be manipulated.

- An BPD has failed to develop the affectional bonds which would allow them to empathize with another's pain.

- From a BPD partner: "It's good to know he's in recovery, because then my own experience doesn't seem like such a waste of life."

- Keep swimming to freedom and healing. You're in the middle of the lake now. If you stop, you'll drown.

- You have had more than enough creepiness in your life. That part's over.

- Once you realize you have given your power away, you can make the decision to take it back.

- All I wanted was someone to grow old with. What I got instead was someone helping me to an early grave.

- A big day in my life was when I decided I needed to be *proactive* instead of *reactive* about this relationship and my own life.

- Living with a BPD is like psychological incarceration – a prisoner of war camp in your own home.

- Treating post traumatic stress disorder is difficult when the trauma isn't *past*. It's hard to get well from your hammer wounds when you're still being hit on the head.

- It's difficult to accept the pain of loving someone who cannot love you, no matter what you do.

- What you are afraid to do is a clear indicator of the next thing to do.

- Some days I'm bursting with outrage, stung with the bitter, unfair circumstances. Still other days, I am grieving as though someone has died. I have never known such melancholy.

- I was so dense, and so hoovered, and so committed … to something that just wasn't there.

- My BPD alternates between denial and despair.

- Greek metaphor for BPD – Trojan horse

- BPD's self-commentary: "I'm better in the abstract."

- Ultimately, you have no choice but to feel what you are feeling.

- Human development progresses in stages. Each time we were unable to resolve the tasks of one developmental stage, those of the next become even more insurmountable. Thus, BPDs are left disabled in many ways.

- Falling out of love is the hardest thing you'll ever do.

- An BPD is limbically challenged. (The limbic system in the brain governs emotions. Medications can calm the limbic system down and reduce the BPD's overreactions.)

- If someone shows you who they are by their actions, *believe* them – the *first* time!

- Knowing about BPD-ism involves a loss of innocence, but it is an essential tool in navigating through society and life.

- Things are not what they seem – they are what they are.

- Life with a BPD can be either a merry-go-round or a roller coaster. With better understanding, we can get off the merry-go-round and move to a roller coaster. At least then there will be a sense of progress.

- BPD-ism: a thought disorder with transitory psychotic episodes

- BPDs don't have friends – they have prisoners.

- Projection – *you're* the one with *my* problem.

- Life with a BPD – soul rape.

- Whatever you are trying to avoid won't go away until you confront it.

- I stayed with him and went back with him because I believe in working things out whenever possible. I was also without adequate knowledge to make a choice. When I obtained the knowledge I needed to see it for what it was, I made a firm decision and stuck with it. End of story.

- Fate is the vengeance of choices unmade.

- Reactions of normal people (having grown up in a loving home) to BPD behavior are shock, *profound* hurt and disorientation. They then leave the relationship.

- There are no mistakes – only lessons.

- BPDs are emotionally numb, which functions for them as emotional self-preservation.

- BPDs are chronically discontent and assume the role of the *Avenger.*

- Co-dependence is an illness of blind denial and self-abandonment.

- "How crazy craziness makes everyone, how irrationally afraid. The madness hidden in each of us, called to, identified, aroused like a lust. And against that the jaw sets. The more I fear my own insanity, the more I must punish yours." – Kate Millett

- If you worry about what *might be,* and wonder what *might have been,* you will ignore what *is.*

- Roadkill stage of the BPD partner – emotionally flattened, feeling dead and repulsive to the world

- Before I met my BPD partner, people called me *Mary Sunshine.*

- Many of us are stuck in *conditional* love, which usually doesn't last and is rather manipulative.

- From Dr. Sam Vaknin (www.malignantselflove.tripod.com) – Educate people to beware of narcissists. Teach them how to identify narcissists, how to cope with them, how to avoid them, and how to divorce them.

- Again from Dr. Sam Vaknin – "Narcissism is the mental epidemic of the 20th century, a plague to be fought by all means."

- To a BPD, it's the innocent and trusting people who are ideal prey.

- BPDs use behavior and gestures to *act* emotional – but there is no emotional correlate, no inner resonance.

- Co-dependents – people who see potential in others and want to encourage it.

- The rates of patient drop-out are high in trials of drugs to combat BPD behavior and thought processes. Unless they become really ill, hit a wall and /or hit bottom, they just don't believe they're ill. They use blame and projection and don't see a reason to tolerate side effects of medications.

- Before you can break out of prison, you must first realize you are locked up.

- Being hoovered can feel good – but it has consequences that *don't* feel good.

- Most BPDs are *stuck* at the developmental age of two.

- A veil has been lifted for the first time in my life. A crazy and confusing existence is finally illuminated. I get it. I understand BPD.

- A few days of bliss, followed by the days from hell.

- I've spent 50 years trying to figure out why there was so much pain in my marriage. Now I know I wasn't the crazy one.

- I'm tired of going into the corner to lick my wounds every time they act up or give the silent treatment.

- Now there is a name for the monster, and I understand the fundamental dynamics.

- I've tried and tried for so long to find happiness in my relationship. I feel like I've been digging for a golden horseshoe in a pile of shit.

- If it was always my fault, now that I'm gone, whose fault is it now?

- She has split images of you, based on whether or not her needs are getting met the way she wants them.

- Whatever you are willing to put up with is exactly what you will have.

- When you live with a BPD, every day is Groundhog Day. We live the same conflicts over and over, just inserting a new trigger issue every so often to give the illusion of variety.

- I'm finally in a place where I understand that she *has* to rage, and she *deserves* to rage. I just won't *engage* her in her rage any more.

- Many of us may be too objective for our own good. I try *so* hard to see the other side and *understand*. Well, I have just *understood* myself right into the depths of hell.

- When you blame others, you give up your power to change.

- The symptoms of BPD-ism are so similar that there are really only two people with BPD – a male and a female – cloned over and over in all our relationships. We're all in BPD relationships with the same person.

- There's a difference between unconditional love and blind, insane tolerance of poor treatment.

- Journals can be good reality tests. Read the awful parts every time you're tempted to get sucked back in. Repeat the following frequently: "This behavior is *not* normal," "This abuse is *not* okay," and "I deserve my own boundaries, emotions, thoughts and happiness."

- A friend asked me if he would still be my friend if he had treated me the way my BPD partner did. I replied that I wouldn't have considered him much of a friend. He said, "Just my point."

- Divorces are final long before they go to court.

- We're *objects* that *should* meet their needs. When we don't do that, then we're split into those *all bad objects* and punished.

- It takes a long time for burns to heal, whether they're outside or inside.

- The more difficult tasks in life are that way because the reward at the end is that much more precious.

- My partner is NBD and OCD, with psychotic tendencies — which is the gift that keeps on giving.

- Personality disorders (PDs), by definition, are disorders of personality. Consequently, they are typified by early onset, pervasive effects, and relatively poor prognosis — it's hard to cure someone of their personality. Nevertheless, there *are* treatments that can help those with PDs learn to cope with their distinctive problems in living.

- BPD's are people known by the place in their brain that's not working properly.

- I knew that I would always have love for my partner. However, there were parts of my life that I *could* not, *dared* not, open to her again, not only because of the pain it would cause me, but because she could not handle those parts — and I could not live without them.

- The one who loves the least controls the relationship.

- The Good Witch in the movie *The Wizard of Oz:* "You've had the power all along."

- The BPD feels like a *victim* (powerless). They may try to over compensate for this by attempting to control others, only to find that they can't, which can substantiate that they *don't* have control … in which case they punish.

- "My land is bare of chattering folk; The clouds are low along the ridges, And sweet's the air with curly smoke From all my burning bridges." – Dorothy Parker

- "Aerodynamically, the bumblebee shouldn't be able to fly, but the bumblebee doesn't know that, so it goes on flying anyway." – Mary Kay Ash, founder of Mary Kay Cosmetics

- "Though we travel the world over to find the beautiful, we must carry it with us or we will find it not." – Ralph Waldo Emerson

DEFINITIONS AND BEHAVIOR DESCRIPTIONS

How do we describe how a BPD acts? How can we put it all into just one nutshell description when BPD's come in so many different shapes, sizes, colors and flavors?

Some explode in rages. Some lurk quietly in the background and then attack. Others withdraw for days, weeks … months. Some control the actions of their partner, even stalking them. There are signs of depression, to the point of attempting suicide sometimes.

Some do all of the above. The list seems endless, twisting and turning the BPD's partner as each new behavior is exhibited.

How do we describe to others the *never knowing* from one minute to the next whether they'll explode at us? How can we tell people how nervous we feel when it gets *quiet*? Are they withdrawing and building up steam for a volcano act? Or are they quietly watching *us*, looking for signs that *we* are leaving?

How do we describe the feeling of having a ticking time bomb in our own home – our supposed-to-be *safe* place? It feels so hopeless sometimes.

~ ~ ~

In 1994, the American Psychiatric Association added to its list of criterion for mental illnesses ten types of personality disorders, all of which result in significant distress and/or negative consequences within the individual. This information was included in its Diagnostic and Statistical Manual of Mental Disorders, Fourth Edition (DSM-IV), Washington, D. C.: American Psychiatric Association, 1994, pp. 650 – 654.

The reader can do additional research to learn about the other eight personality disorders, but in *Breaking Free from Boomerang Love*, the two personality disorders of borderline personality disorder and narcissism are the focal points. Speaking about borderline personality disorder without including narcissism would present an incomplete picture.

Therefore, included below are descriptions of both the borderline personality disorder and the narcissistic personality disorder.

Borderline Personality Disorder

Besides the author's web site at www.boomeranglove.com, other excellent web sites for additional information about borderline personality disorder are www.borderlineresearch.org, www.tara4bpd.org, www.ybrt.org, www.mental-health-today.com, and www.bpdcentral.com.

According to the DSM-IV, persons with borderline personality disorder display a pervasive pattern of instability of interpersonal relationships, self-image, and affects and marked impulsivity beginning by early adulthood and present in a variety of contexts, as indicated by five (or more) of the following:

1. Frantic efforts to avoid real or imagined abandonment. (Note: Do not include suicidal or self-mutilating behavior covered in Criterion 5.)
2. A pattern of unstable and intense interpersonal relationships characterized by alternating between extremes of idealization and devaluation
3. Identity disturbance: markedly and persistently unstable self-image or sense of self
4. Impulsivity in at least two areas that are potentially self-damaging (e.g., spending, sex, substance abuse, reckless driving, binge eating). (Note: Do not include suicidal or self-mutilating behavior covered in Criterion 5.)
5. Recurrent suicidal behavior, gestures, or threats, or self-mutilating behavior
6. Affective instability due to a marked reactivity of mood (e.g., intense episodic dysphoria, irritability, or anxiety usually lasting a few hours and only rarely more than a few days
7. Chronic feelings of emptiness
8. Inappropriate, intense anger or difficulty controlling anger (e.g., frequent displays of temper, constant anger, recurrent physical fights)
9. Transient, stress-related paranoid ideation or severe dissociative symptoms.

The DSM-IV goes on to say:

The essential feature of Borderline Personality Disorder is a pervasive pattern of instability of interpersonal relationships, self-image, and affects, and marked impulsivity that begins by early adulthood and is present in a variety of contexts.

Individuals with Borderline Personality Disorder make frantic efforts to avoid real or imagined abandonment (Criterion 1). The perception of impending separation or rejection, or the loss of external structure, can lead to profound changes in self-image, affect, cognition, and behavior. These individuals are very sensitive to environmental circumstances. They experience intense abandonment fears and inappropriate anger even when faced with a realistic time-limited separation or when there are unavoidable changes in plans (e.g., sudden despair in reaction to a clinician's announcing the end of the hour; panic or fury when someone important to them is just a few minutes late or must cancel an appointment). They may believe that this "abandonment" implies they are "bad". These abandonment fears are related to an intolerance of being alone and a need to have other people with them. Their frantic efforts to avoid abandonment may include impulsive action such as self-mutilating or suicidal behaviors, which are described separately in Criterion 5.

Individuals with Borderline Personality Disorder have a pattern of unstable and intense relationships (Criterion 2). They may idealize potential caregivers or lovers at the first or second meeting, demand to spend a lot of time together, and share the most intimate details early in a relationship. However, they may switch quickly from idealizing other people to devaluing them, feeling that the other person does not care enough, does not give enough, is not "there" enough. These individuals can empathize with and nurture other people, but only with the expectation that the other person will "be there" in return to meet their own needs on demand. These individuals are prone to sudden and dramatic shifts in their view of others, who may alternately be seen as beneficent supports or as cruelly punitive. Such shifts often reflect disillusionment with a caregiver whose nurturing qualities had been idealized or whose rejection or abandonment is expected.

There may be an identity disturbance characterized by markedly and persistently unstable self-image or sense of self (Criterion 3). There are sudden and dramatic shifts in self-image, characterized by shifting goals, values, and vocational aspirations. There may be sudden changes in opinions and plans about career, sexual identity, values, and types of friends. These individuals may suddenly change from the role of a needy supplicant for help to a righteous avenger of past mistreatment. Although they usually have a self-image that is based on being bad or evil, individuals with this disorder may at times have feelings that they do not exist at all. Such experiences usually occur in situations in which the individual feels a lack of meaningful relationship, nurturing and support. These individuals may show worse performance in unstructured work or school situations.

Individuals with this disorder display impulsivity in at least two areas that are potentially self-damaging (Criterion 4). They may gamble, spend money irresponsibly, binge eat, abuse substances, engage in unsafe sex, or drive recklessly.

Individuals with Borderline Personality Disorder display recurrent suicidal behavior, gestures, or threats, or self-mutilating behavior (Criterion 5). Completed suicide occurs in eight to ten per cent of such individuals, and self-mutilative acts (e.g., cutting or burning) and suicide threats and attempts are very common. Recurrent suicidality is often the reason that these individuals present for help. These self-destructive acts are usually precipitated by threats of separation or rejection or by expectations that they assume increased responsibility. Self-mutilation may occur during dissociative experiences and often brings relief by reaffirming the ability to feel or by expiating the individual's sense of being evil.

Individuals with Borderline Personality Disorder may display affective instability that is due to a marked reactivity of mood (e.g., intense episodic dysphoria, irritability, or anxiety usually lasting few hours and only rarely more than a few days) (Criterion 6). The basic dysphoric mood of those with borderline personality disorder is often disrupted by periods of anger, panic, or despair and is rarely relieved by periods of well-being or satisfaction.

These episodes may reflect the individual's extreme reactivity troubled by chronic feelings of emptiness (Criterion 7). Easily bored, they may constantly seek something to do.

Individuals with Borderline Personality Disorder frequently express inappropriate, intense anger or have difficulty controlling their anger (Criterion 8). They may display extreme sarcasm, enduring bitterness, or verbal outbursts. The anger is often elicited when a caregiver or lover is seen as neglectful, withholding, uncaring, or abandoning. Such expression of anger are often followed by shame and guilt and contribute to the feeling they have of being evil.

During periods of extreme stress, transient paranoid ideation or dissociative symptoms (e.g., depersonalization) may occur (Criterion 9), but these are generally of insufficient severity or duration to warrant an additional diagnosis. These episodes occur most frequently in response to a real or imagined abandonment. Symptoms tend to be transient, lasting minutes or hours. The real or perceived return of the caregiver's nurturance may result in a remission of symptoms.

Associated Features and Disorders

Individuals with Borderline Personality Disorder may have a pattern of undermining themselves at the moment a goal is about to be realized (e.g., dropping out of school just before graduation; regressing severely after a discussion of how well therapy is going; destroying a good relationship just when it is clear that the relationship could last). Some individuals develop psychotic-like symptoms (e.g., hallucinations, body-image distortions, ideas of reference, and hypnotic phenomena) during times of stress. Individuals with this disorder may feel more secure with transitional objects (i.e., a pet or inanimate possession) than in interpersonal relationships. Premature death from suicide may occur in individuals with this disorder, especially in those with co-occurring Mood Disorders or Substance-Related Disorders. Physical handicaps may result from self-inflicted abuse behaviors or failed suicide attempts. Recurrent job losses, interrupted education, and broken marriages are common. Physical and sexual abuse, neglect, hostile conflict, and early parental loss or separation are more common in the childhood histories of those with borderline personality disorder. Common co-occurring Axis I disorders include Mood Disorders, Substance-Related Disorders, Eating Disorders (notably Bulimia), Post

Traumatic Stress Disorder, and Attention-Deficit/Hyperactivity Disorder. Borderline Personality Disorder also frequently co-occurs with other Personality Disorders.

Specific Culture, Age, and Gender Features

The pattern of behavior seen in Borderline Personality Disorder has been identified in many settings around the world. Adolescents and young adults with identity problems (especially when accompanied by substance abuse) may transiently display behaviors that misleadingly give the impression of Borderline Personality Disorder. Such situations are characterized by emotional instability, "existential" dilemmas, uncertainty, anxiety-provoking choices, conflicts about sexual orientation, and competing social pressures to decide on careers.

Borderline Personality Disorder is diagnosed predominantly (about 75 per cent) in females.

Prevalence

The prevalence of Borderline Personality Disorder is estimated to be about two per cent of the general population, about ten per cent among individuals seen in outpatient mental health clinics, and about 20 per cent among psychiatric inpatients. It ranges from 30 per cent to 60 per cent among clinical populations with Personality Disorders.

Course

There is considerable variability in the course of Borderline Personality Disorder. The most common pattern is one of chronic instability in early adulthood, with episodes of serious affective and impulsive dyscontrol and high levels of use of health and mental health resources. The impairment from the disorder and the risk of suicide are greatest in the young adult years and gradually wane with advancing age. During their 30's and 40's, the majority of individuals with this disorder attain greater stability in their relationships and vocational functioning.

FAMILIAL PATTERN

Borderline Personality Disorder is about five times more common among first-degree biological relatives of those with the disorder than in the general population. There is also an increased familial risk for Substance-Related Disorders, Antisocial Personality Disorder, and Mood Disorders.

DIFFERENTIAL DIAGNOSIS

Borderline Personality Disorder often co-occurs with Mood Disorders, and when criteria for both are met, both may be diagnosed. Because the cross-sectional presentation of Borderline Personality Disorder can be mimicked by an episode of Mood Disorder, the clinician should avoid giving an additional diagnosis of Borderline Personality Disorder based only on cross-sectional presentation without having documented that the pattern of behavior has an early onset and a long-standing course.

Other Personality Disorders may be confused with Borderline Personality Disorder because they have certain features in common. It is, therefore, important to distinguish among these disorders based on differences in their characteristic features. However, if an individual has personality features that meet criteria for one or more Personality Disorders in addition to Borderline Personality Disorder, all can be diagnosed.

Although Histrionic Personality Disorder can also be characterized by attention seeking, manipulative behavior, and rapidly shifting emotions, Borderline Personality Disorder is distinguished by self-destructiveness, angry disruptions in close relationships, and chronic feelings of deep emptiness and loneliness.

Paranoid ideas or illusions may be present in both Borderline Personality Disorder and Schizotypal Personality Disorder, but these symptoms are more transient, interpersonally reactive, and responsive to external structuring in Borderline Personality Disorder.

duplicate

Although Paranoid Personality Disorder and Narcissistic Personality Disorder may also be characterized by an angry reaction to minor stimuli, the relative stability of self-image as well as the relative lack of self-destructiveness, impulsivity, and abandonment concerns distinguish these disorders from Borderline Personality Disorder.

Although Antisocial Personality Disorder and Borderline Personality Disorder are both characterized by manipulative behavior, individuals with Antisocial Personality Disorder are manipulative to gain profit, power, or some other material gratification, whereas the goal in Borderline Personality Disorder is directed more toward gaining the concern of caretakers.

Both Dependent Personality Disorder and Borderline Personality Disorder are characterized by fear of abandonment. However, the individual with Borderline Personality Disorder reacts to abandonment with feelings of emotional emptiness, rage, and demands, whereas the individual with Dependent Personality Disorder reacts with increasing appeasement and submissiveness and urgently seeks a replacement relationship to provide care giving and support. Borderline Personality Disorder can further be distinguished from Dependent Personality Disorder by the typical pattern of unstable and intense relationships.

NARCISSISTIC PERSONALITY DISORDER

Dr. Sam Vaknin's web site http://malignantselflove.tripod.com is an excellent source for additional information about narcissism.

The common traits of narcissism can be distilled as follows:

- An obvious self-focus in interpersonal exchanges
- Problems in sustaining satisfying relationships
- Lack of psychological awareness
- Difficulty with empathy
- Problems distinguishing the self from others
- Hypersensitivity to any slights or imagined insults
- Lack of emotional depth and ability to feel sadness; and vulnerability to shame rather than guilt.

According to the DSM-IV, display of five of the following nine behaviors certifies a person as having narcissistic personality disorder:

- Feels grandiose and self-important – Exaggerates achievements and talents to the point of lying; demands to be recognized as superior without commensurate achievements
- Is obsessed with fantasies of unlimited success, fame, fearsome power or omnipotence, unequalled brilliance (the cerebral narcissist), bodily beauty or sexual performance (the somatic narcissist), or ideal, everlasting, all-conquering love or passion
- Firmly convinced that he or she is unique and, being special, can only be understood by, should only be treated by, or associate with, other special or unique, or high-status people (or institutions)
- Requires excessive admiration, adulation, attention and affirmation – or, failing that, wishes to be feared and to be notorious (narcissistic supply)
- Feels entitled. Expects unreasonable or special and favorable priority treatment.
- Demands automatic and full compliance with his or her expectations
- Is interpersonally exploitative – uses others to achieve his or her own ends
- Devoid of empathy. Is unable or unwilling to identify with or acknowledge the feelings and needs of others
- Constantly envious of others or believes that they feel the same about him or her
- Arrogant, haughty behaviors or attitudes coupled with rage when frustrated, contradicted, or confronted

RESOURCES AND TOOLS

The following resources have been arranged in a specific, chronological order to guide our journey of education, understanding and healing.

Section I contains what I call our *Starter Kit.* Obtain all four books – or find them at your local library – but read all of them. Each book gives us a different piece to the jigsaw puzzle picture we're trying to put together out of the craziness in our lives.

Section II adds the very necessary element of going inside ourselves to discover our *own* behaviors which possibly led us into these painful relationships – and may be keeping us trapped in them.

Section III: When you're ready to go deeper, inside your own psyche and that of your partner, dig in here. There's much to feast on. Take what you like and leave the rest. By this point in your journey, you should be getting more clear in your mind as to what your personal pathway will be – staying with, or leaving, your BPD. One or another of the books in this section may help you cement that resolve.

> "Sometimes our light goes out but is blown into flame by another human being. Each of us owes deepest thanks to those who have rekindled this light."
>
> – Albert Schweitzer

I offer profound thanks to the authors and other people listed below for their compassionate efforts to shine a light in the darkness for those lost in the BPD forest of pain. One light leads to another … to another … to another. And then one day we're finally out of the incomprehensible forest and into the sunshine of reality and truth, drinking in the deliciousness of the ocean, feeling the warm sand between our toes, relaxing at last. Deepest gratitude indeed.

SECTION I

I Hate You, Don't Leave Me: Understanding the Borderline Personality. 1989. Jerold J. Kreisman, M. D., and Hal Straus. New York, NY: Avon Books, division of The Hearst Corporation

Written in 1989, this is the first book for laypersons regarding borderline personality disorder. Read this handy little paperback first. It says it like it is and draws clear circles around the symptoms and behaviors.

It has been criticized by some members of the mental health profession, because primary emphasis is put on educating the reader as to what BPD *looks* like. But this is exactly what *we* need. Treatment and help for the BPD come *after* we rescue *ourselves*.

In my journey, I spent *years* sugar-coating my BPD partner's behavior, giving him excuses for the abuse he hurled at me, and forgiving him endlessly. When I began my learning process about BPD, I needed to know *clearly* what the behavior was. I needed validation that my pain was *real*. I needed to know *the name of my pain*.

Stop Walking On Eggshells: Taking Your Life Back When Someone You Care About Has Borderline Personality Disorder. 1998. Paul T. Mason, M.S., and Randi Kreger. Oakland, CA: New Harbinger Publications, Inc.

Fast forward nine years to 1998. The Diagnostic and Statistical Manual IV (DSM-IV) – the *Bible* for the mental health profession for diagnostic criteria – has added personality disorders in a special, Axis II section. And the Internet has arrived.

Through the interaction of a caring Internet community of partners of BPDs, communicating with each other electronically by way of emails, Randi Kreger began to understand the disorder from the *inside out*. Along with social worker Paul Mason, she co-wrote this book (known as SWOE to the borderline personality disorder partners on the Internet).

For us non-mental health professionals, it's a very understandable, easy read that clearly explains the *ways* that BPs behave and communicate – and *why*. It's a good, nuts-and-bolts, *how-to* type of book that adds specific strategies partners can use to cope with the borderline personality behaviors.

The Stop Walking on Eggshells Workbook. 2002. Randi Kreger and James Paul Shirley, LMSW. Oakland, CA: New Harbinger Publications, Inc.

Just what it says – a workbook to help us better implement the tools in the above book of the same name.

Understanding The Borderline Mother: Helping Her Children Transcend the Intense, Unpredictable and Volatile Relationship. 2000. Christine Ann Lawson. Northvale, NJ: Jason Aronson, Inc.

Don't be put off by the size of this book. It's hands-down the most clearly-written, easily understandable, most gut-wrenching book on BPD available for the layperson today. As detached and healed as I am now from my deceased BPD mother – and my BPD partner – I found myself crying in many parts of this book.

The clarity of Dr. Lawson's vision of BPD and its effect on those interacting with them is astonishing. Through this book, I touched again those parts of myself that were still hurting over the way I was treated by my mother and saw even more distinctly why I was such easy fodder for a relationship with a borderline.

Using characters from Grimm's Fairy Tales (the witch in Hansel & Gretel, the mother who sends her children into the woods), to Alice in Wonderland (the Queen: "Off with her head!"), and Cinderella (helpless and abused), she simply and powerfully paints a picture of the pain that comes our way when we live with a person who has this disorder. Dr. Lawson is equally compassionate to the BPD, empathically urging early intervention to try to protect the children.

It's important to note that even though the title of the book mentions *mothers,* the borderline picture depicted in this book fits both females *and* males. Partners of male BPDs will also appreciate this book.

SECTION II

I never saw myself more clearly than in the 12-Step program called Co-Dependents Anonymous (CoDA). I'm in my eighth year of what's called "recovery" in these groups, and I still drop into a meeting occasionally – for a "booster." Slipping back into old habits such as trying to *fix* other people's problems, over-giving of myself, and not taking good care of myself emotionally are things I need to be continuously on guard against.

I still treasure the friendships of the people who helped me through those torturous years and provided the emotional support I needed so desperately.

And then there's the Internet. It's really crucial that we connect with others in the same situation we're in – for understanding and support. It was an incredible revelation for me to find a whole community chat board of people on the Internet dealing with the same behaviors in their partners that I was wrestling with. Everyone on the community board was like me – struggling to understand, to protect themselves and their families, and to *heal* from BPD relationships. I had thought I was the only person in the world dealing with such craziness. Until I found that board, I felt completely alone and defeated.

Another valuable element for healing is time spent with a professional psychotherapist. I remember reading somewhere that in the course of our lives, given only our own personal experience and knowledge, we'll all get from point A ... to point B ... to point C. But it may take us 20 years! A therapist is trained to help us see and understand the reality of what's happening in our lives and to support us as we make the steps to move more rapidly through our A, B and C points.

We may also need some *medication* to weather the overwhelming emotions we're experiencing. I see today's wonderful chemicals as bridges from one side of hell to the other. When we get out, we don't need them anymore. But while we're *in* hell, they're life savers.

A word of caution here, though. Be very selective in the therapist you choose. It's my understanding that most of the therapists who got their training *before the mid-1990s* do *not* know how to diagnose and/or treat personality disorders. They simply didn't learn about it in school.

Psychologist Marsha Linehan, Ph. D., of Seattle, Washington, has created a new treatment program for these problems called Dialectical Behavioral Therapy. Dr. Linehan has been training therapists with her method through seminars, books and training manuals since 1993.

Dr. Linehan's web site through the University of Washington is http://faculty.washington.edu/linehan. It can be used to locate DBT-trained pychotherapists in your area, in addition to finding upcoming DBT training seminars for mental health professionals.

Dr. Linehan's books on DBT are included in Section III.

Also, in obtaining a therapist, make sure the one you choose has at least a Master's in counseling or clinical psychology. They need this level of training, *at the minimum* to be able to diagnose and treat borderline personality disorder.

It's also a good idea to check the credentials of the potential therapist. It's best if they're NCC-credentialed (certified by the National Board for Certified Counselors). This board has a website where you can click to "Find a Therapist."

Check also to see if the potential therapist is licensed by the state you live in. The NBCC or NCC exam is usually the exam that states mandate for licensure.

If you'd prefer a therapist with doctorate level training, you would want someone with a degree in clinical psychology. They're covered by the American Psychological Association, which also has a website. Here you'll find doctors of psychiatry, as well as Ph.Ds

Co-Dependents Anonymous Support Groups

Go to "search" mode on your computer for this subject, and you'll find 12-Step programs very much alive and well on the Internet. There should be enough information to connect you with a group meeting near you.

Or call your local Alcoholic Anonymous or Al-Anon group for help in locating Co-Dependents Anonymous in your area.

Al-Anon Family Support Groups

I also spent a fair amount of time in Al-Anon, as there were addiction issues with my now deceased mother. I found the meetings and reading materials absolutely invaluable in helping me "detach" from the hurtful BPD behavior and therefore the emotional pain that was coming my way from my partner.

The Al-Anon message is clear: We *can* learn to live a happy, joyous life – whether or not our partners ever get well.

Co-Dependents Anonymous Books

The Language of Letting Go – Daily Meditations for Codependents. 1990. Melody Beattie. New York, NY: HarperCollins.

When I first read this book, I practically went into meltdown. I finally touched the injured part of myself that was so terrified of being abandoned emotionally – and all the behavioral issues I was trapped in as a result of that fear.

My BPD partner was terrified of abandonment, and so he punished me ... and *I* was terrified of abandonment and so I clung to his ankles – even *though* he punished me! What a pair we were – it's called the "Dance of Death" in the 12-Step programs.

Melody Beattie talks about "not setting ourselves up to be victims" and "owning our power to take care of ourselves."

Written in the form of daily meditations, I can't recommend this book highly enough.

Codependent No More. 1987. Melody Beattie. Center City, Minn: Hazelden

Melody Beattie's first book on codependency. Read this if you'd like more of an over-all view.

Codependents' Guide to the Twelve Steps – How to Find the Right Program For You and Apply Each of the Twelve Steps to Your Own Issues. 1992. Melody Beattie. New York, NY: Fireside/Parkside, div. of Simon & Schuster, Inc.

All of the *anonymous* programs are structured around the original *Twelve Steps* of Alcoholics Anonymous – an inspired program of guided, step-by-step healing. The First Step is as crucial to partners of BPDs as it is to recovering alcoholics – the personal surrender to the knowledge that we're "powerless over others (alcoholics say 'alcohol') and that our lives have become unmanageable."

Melody Beattie takes each of the Twelve Steps and highlights the issues in them to facilitate healing for codependents – focusing on the traps of caretaking, shame, controlling, obsessing, victimization, and neglect of self-responsibility that we can fall into.

This book helps people learn to stop asking, "How can I help *others?*" and start asking, "How can I help *myself?*"

INTERNET

LandofOz@yahoogroups.com

To subscribe, email LandofOz-subscribe@yahoogroups.com

Remember the movie *Wizard of Oz?* Dorothy whisked off to a land where nothing makes sense, an evil witch wants to hurt and punish her, and monkeys fly out of trees. Not to mention the fraud behind the screen, who pretends to be an "expert" who could help her and turns out to have absolutely *no* ability to relieve the problems she had.

And, of course, Dorothy discovering that she had always had the power to set herself free (her red shoes) – she just didn't know it.

This online support group is named the Land Of Oz (LOO) because as partners of BPDs, we feel like Dorothy – things happen that puzzle and confuse us, we're hurt and feel threatened … and *no one* seems to be able to understand what we're dealing with or help us.

The goal of this site is to "get back to Kansas" – back to a *normal* life, where we can feel safe and loved consistently.

Hundreds of people have held hands technologically and shared their stories and knowledge with each other on this site, urging each other on and holding each others' noses above water. We call each other "Ozzies."

In addition, this is the only online support group I'm aware of that has a licensed clinician as moderator. Elyce M. Benham, MS, NCC, CCFC, LPC, volunteers her time to answer the posts. Affectionately known on this site as "Glenda, the Good Witch," she has 19 years of experience working with BPD. She currently works in the Acute Patient Unit at a Pacific Northwest Hospital. Her advice is priceless.

Informational Web Sites

www.ybrt.org – Land of Oz information site
- Resources for individuals and families dealing with BPD
- How to join online support group "Land of Oz" (LandofOz@yahoo.groups.com)
- Book lists
- Important insights for someone planning to leave someone with BPD

http://faculty.washington.edu/linehan – Dr. Marshal Linehan's website

www.tara4bpd.org – National organization promoting support groups

www.mental-health-today.com – support, information and resources

www.palace.net/~llama/psych/ – self-help for self-injury

www.borderlineresearch.org

www.borderlinemothers.com – information

http://malignantlove.tripod.com – support and information regarding narcissistic personality disorder

www.psyweb.com – wide variety of mental health topics

www.mentalhealth.com – wide variety of mental health topics

www.adaa.org – Anxiety Disorders of America home page

http://freedomfromfear.com – support and information regarding anxiety disorders

www.borderlinepersonalitydisorder.com – National Education Association for Borderline Personality Disorder home page

www.PDAN.org — Personality Disorders Network

Other sites are available by *search* mode on your computer. Search for "borderline personality disorder" and "narcissist."

SECTION III

The Emotionally Abused Woman – Overcoming Destructive Patterns and Reclaiming Yourself. 1990. Beverly Engel, M.F.C.C. New York: Ballantine Books, div. of Random House

Written before Co-Dependents Anonymous took off across the country, Beverly Engel's book fits right in with the behavior descriptions of personality disorders and the need for healing of those in relationships with them. This is an excellent book for sorting out how in the heck we got into such painful relationships in the first place.

However, Ms. Engel doesn't mince words about the types of people who end up emotionally abused, the kinds of people they're attracted to, and why. Don't read this book if you're not yet comfortable looking at yourself honestly.

The chapter on "Should You Stay or Should You Leave" is very helpful, as is the one on "If You Decide to Stay."

The Betrayal Bond – Breaking Free of Exploitive Relationships. 1997. Patrick J. Carnes, Ph. D. Deerfield Beach, FLA: Health Communications, Inc.

Dr. Patrick Carnes was also the victim of Boomerang Love, only he calls it the Charlie Brown and Lucy Van Pelt syndrome. Each time, Charlie Brown is sucked back in again, believing that the football will really be there to be kicked.

However, Dr. Carnes believes the on-again, off-again nature of relationships with abusive people is borne of something he calls a "betrayal bond," or bonding with people who are very hurtful to us and thereafter remaining loyal to them, despite betrayal and exploitation.

Dr. Carnes says that when the right chemistry of loving care, alternated with fear, terror, threats, degrading behavior, or violence is created, a "trauma bond" is formed. Trauma bonds are very difficult to perceive and even harder to break. Trauma bonding based in childhood is frequently at the core of our behavior as adults when we again trauma bond with abusive partners.

Dr. Carnes details strategies to identify early patterns of trauma bonding and how to trace them into our current relationships. Also included are steps for action and recovery.

Black Swan – The Twelve Lessons of Abandonment Recovery – Featuring: The Allegory of the Little Girl on the Rock. 1999. Susan Anderson, C.S.W. Huntington, New York: Rock Foundations Press

Written by psychotherapist Susan Anderson one year before her *Journey from Abandonment to Healing*, this little book is a night light – a teddy-bear-book to take to bed with us when the intensity of our abandonment threatens to overwhelm us.

In the story of a little girl who goes on a walk in the woods with a father who never returns from picking huckleberries, Ms. Anderson weaves a careful story of growth and recovery that helps us get in touch with our oldest and truest feelings left over from childhood. She then moves onward to connect these feelings with the intensity of the experience of our current abandonment wounds.

The "twelve lessons" delivered by the Black Swan are the actual methods Ms. Anderson recommends for recovery.

Reading the longer book that came after this one will reveal lots of good information and help, but this is the book to carry in our pockets for those moments when we need a quick "pick-me-up" to get through the day … the next hour … the next minute.

The Journey from Abandonment to Healing: Surviving Through – and Recovering From – the Five Stages that Accompany the Loss of Love. 2000. Susan Anderson, C.S.W. New York, NY: The Berkley Publishing Group, a division of Penguin Putnam, Inc.

The searing pain of abandonment and aloneness. Whether it's the end of a relationship, the death of a loved one or any other deeply-felt emotional loss, we still feel abandoned.

In her work as a psychotherapist, Susan Anderson has specialized in helping people with loss, heartbreak, and abandonment for more than 25 years. She calls it "abandonment recovery." It was wonderfully comforting for me to read this book and find where I was in Ms. Anderson's *Five Stages of Abandonment*.

In addition to addressing early childhood issues of abandonment, Ms. Anderson also shows recent findings from the field of brain science that shed new light on the biological and chemical processes that underlie our emotional response to loss. (Further evidence supporting my statement in Section II that "we may also need some medication to weather the overwhelming emotions we're experiencing.")

The Verbally Abusive Relationship – How to Recognize It and How to Respond. 1992. Patricia Evans. Holbrook, MA: Bob Adams, Inc.

Patricia Evans believes that psychological repression is maintained by verbal manipulation and coercion. It's a form of control that perpetuates itself as long as it remains unrecognized.

Verbal abuse is described as "a kind of battery which doesn't leave evidence comparable to the bruises of physical battery." However, it can be just as painful, and recovery can take much longer.

Ms. Evans provides check lists of behaviors to help recognize verbal abuse, along with the feelings that occur when we are abused in that manner. Also helpful are the sections on how to respond to verbally abusive behavior.

Although Ms. Evans doesn't mention personality disorders specifically, I believe many personality-disordered people are definitely verbally abusive. If you're still on the fence, not sure whether power is being subtly used against you, or still hoping that maybe your partner "just had a bad day," this is a good book for you.

Emotional Blackmail – When the People in Your Life Use Fear, Obligation and Guilt to Manipulate You. 1997. Susan Forward, Ph. D., and Donna Frazier. New York, NY: HarperCollins Publishers, Inc.

"If you really loved me ... ."

"After all I've done for you ... ."

"How can you be so selfish?"

If you feel trapped in your relationship by fear, obligation or guilt (FOG), this book will help you see and understand the mental extortion being used against you.

Concise advice is presented on how to recognize all our hot buttons that emotional blackmailers push (fear of abandonment, fear of anger, fear of change and fear of disapproval, in addition to obligation and guilt).

Step-by-step advice is offered on how to strengthen ourselves to withstand the behavior, plus strategies on how to respond effectively. Lots of assistance here to help us break out of the chains holding us back.

Psychotherapy and Treatment

How Therapists Diagnose: Seeing Through the Psychiatric Eye – Professional Secrets You Deserve to Know and How They Affect You and Your Family. 1994. Dr. Bruce Hamstra. New York: St. Martin's Griffin

Dr. Bruce Hamstra states in this book that for years, he hid behind *professional ethics* and the commonly held belief by the mental health professionals that *untrained individuals* (the general public – you and me) could potentially misuse and abuse the *release of professional information* on how diagnoses are made.

After a close friend of his ended up in the hospital with a life-threatening cancerous tumor, Dr. Hamstra observed how easily the treating doctors informed his friend about how the diagnosis was made, what the medical tests meant, and how his treatment was being determined.

In other words, his friend's doctors were willing to be held accountable for the diagnosis and treatment they were providing.

The absurdity of the position of the mental health profession in not providing the same sort of information to its clients became obvious to Dr. Hamstra, and this book was born. He believes that if a client asks about their diagnosis, particularly if it involves the "more nebulous personality disorders," they have a right to full disclosure and accountability from the professional they've consulted.

In order to help mental health consumers be actively involved not only in their treatment, but in their diagnosis as well, Dr. Hamstra reveals the new diagnostic guidelines therapists use to make assessments, how insurance companies pay for mental health claims, and questions to ask your therapist to make them accountable. He shows the difficulties therapists have with diagnoses, as some *overdiagnose* in order to justify treatment to insurance companies. Others *underdiagnose* because they don't want the client to be labeled by a more severe diagnosis.

Much more is offered in this book than can be detailed here, but know that it's a real eye-opener for "consumers" like us. It's an excellent book to keep handy if you decide to wade into the mental health world.

Eclipses – Behind the Borderline Personality Disorder. 1998. Melissa Ford Thornton. Madison, AL: Monte Sano Publishing

Melissa Thornton describes the world of the borderline as "a scary place, where logic as most people know it, is eclipsed."

Ms. Thornton is a self-described borderline. This book chronicles her journey of treatment for this disorder with Dialectical Behavioral Therapy (created by Dr. Marsha Linehan of the University of Washington in Seattle, Washington). Ms. Thornton was an inpatient at Highland Hospital in Asheville, North Carolina, one of the cutting-edge hospitals in the United States using this technique.

Both saddening and inspiring, this book offers direction and hope for those struggling with this disorder.

Lost in the Mirror – An Inside Look at Borderline Personality Disorder. 2001. Richard Moskovitz, M. D. Lanham, Maryland: Taylor Trade Publishing, a division of the Rowman & Littlefield Publishing Group

Very empathically presented, Dr. Richard Moskovitz attempts to "create a living picture" of the world of the borderline's relationships and feelings, along with a pathway for recovery.

In Dr. Moskovitz' words: "For years, we have kept your diagnosis secret from you for fear that you would be wounded and flee. ... This book is intended to let you in on the secret. ... It is my hope that the understanding that comes from this book will enable you to talk honestly about your feelings. ... This book is also intended to show you how healing occurs."

The Angry Heart – Overcoming Borderline and Addictive Disorders. 1997. Joseph Santoro, Ph. D., and Ronald Cohen, Ph. D. Oakland, CA: New Harbinger Publications

A workbook of healing for borderlines, it offers a good explanation of borderline personality disorder, its causes and symptoms. The feelings, behaviors and "thinking" processes of the borderline are presented in a way that's easily understood.

Recovery exercises, behavior contracts, reinforcement charts, affirmations, self-soothing activities, visualizations, counter- conditioning – lots of tools here to help borderlines ... *if* they want help.

The Search for the Real Self – Unmasking the Personality Disorders of Our Age. 1990. James F. Masterson, M. D. New York, NY: The Free Press, division of Simon & Schuster, Inc.

Dr. Masterson is the authority most often quoted by mental health professionals regarding personality disorders. In this book, he refers primarily to the borderline and narcissistic personality disorders.

This is an excellent book on the development of the "self" – the person we become as an adult. Dr. Masterson describes the "False Self" and the "Real Self." These concepts are extremely important for partners of BPDs, as we struggle daily to deal with the "Dr. Jekyll and Mr. Hyde" aspects of our partners. And in the depths of our grief of whether or not to stay in relationships with our BPD, it's the surrender to the acceptance of the real, underlying nature of our partner (the personality disorder we didn't know existed) that causes the most pain.

After carefully probing the key aspects of fear of abandonment and fear of intimacy, Dr. Masterson details the psychotherapy he recommends for BPD and NPD.

Much deeper than other books on the subject, this book is still very understandable by laypersons if they already have a good understanding of personality disorders.

Cognitive – Behavioral Treatment of BPD. 1993. Marsha Linehan, Ph. D. New York, NY: Guilford Press

Skills Training Manual for Treating BPD. 1993. Marsha Linehan, Ph. D. New York, NY: Guilford Press

Both of these books are written on an academic level for mental health professionals.

Dr. Linehan's website through the University of Washington is www.behavioraltech.com. It can be used to locate DBT- trained psychotherapists in your area, in addition to finding upcoming DBT training seminars for mental health professionals.

Don't Let Your Emotions Run Your Life – How Dialectical Behavior Therapy Can Put You in Control. 2003. Scott E. Spradlin, M. A. Oakland, CA: New Harbinger Publications, Inc.

A self-help workbook to learn how to be more skillful in dealing with our emotions.

Change Your Brain, Change Your Life. 1998. Daniel G. Amen, M. D. New York, NY: Times Books

With Dr. Amen's state-of-the-art brain imaging technology, he has spent the last decade helping thousands of people understand that the way their brains are wired can affect their thoughts and emotions. With "brain prescriptions" of cognitive exercises, nutrition, and medication, Dr. Amen has been helping his clients enhance their brain function and heal their emotional problems.

Surviving the Borderline Parent – How to Heal Your Childhood Wounds and Build Trust,Boundaries, and Self-Esteem. 2003. Roth and Friedman. Oakland, CA: New Harbinger Publications, Inc.

OTHER BOOKS OF INTEREST

When Anger Hurts Your Kids – A Parent's Guide. 1996. M. McKay, P. Fanning, K. Paleg and D. Landis. Oakland, CA: New Harbinger Publications

In the Name of the Child – A Developmental Approach to Understanding and Helping Children of Conflicted and Violent Divorce. 1997. J. A. Johnston and V. Roseby. New York, NY: The Free Press, division of Simon & Schuster

Ashes to Ashes ... Families to Dust – False Accusations of Child Abuse – A Road Map for Survivors. 1996. D. Tong. Tampa, FLA: FamRights Press

Fathers' Rights. 1997. J. M. Leving and K. A. Dachman. New York, NY: BasicBooks

but I love him: Protecting Your Teen Daughter from Conrolling, Abusive Dating Relationships. 2000. Dr. Jill Murray. New York, NY: Regan Books, an imprint of Harper-Collins.

Destructive Relationships. 2002. Dr. Jill Murray. San Diego, CA: Jodere Group, Inc.

Why Is It Always About You? 2003. Sandy Hotchkiss. Free Press.

The Good Divorce: Keeping Your Family Together When Your Marriage Comes Apart. 1998. Constance Ahrons, Ph. D. New York, NY: HarperCollins Publishers, Inc.

Mom's House, Dad's House: Making Two Homes for Your Child. 1997. Isolina Ricci, Ph. D. New York, NY: Simon & Schuster, Inc.

It's Not Your Fault, Koko Bear: Osread-Together Book for Parents and Young Children During Divorce. 1998. Vicki Lansky. Minnetonka, MN: Book Peddlers.

What About the Kids? Raising Your Children Before, During and After the Divorce. 2003. Judith S. Wallerstein and Sandra Blakeslee. New York, NY: Hyperion

Woulda, Coulda, Shoulda: Overcoming Regrets, Mistakes and Missed Opportunities. 1990. Dr. Arthur Freeman and Rose Dewolf. New York, NY: HarperCollins Publishers, Inc.

How You Can Survive When They're Depressed: Living and Coping with Depression Fallout. 1998. Anne Sheffield. New York, NY: **Three Rivers Press**

Boundaries: Where You End and I Begin. 1993. Anne Katherine, MA. New York, NY: Parkside Publishing Corporation

When Your Lover Is a Liar: Healing the Wounds of Deception and Betrayal. 2000. Susan Forward, Ph. D., and Donna Frazier. New York, NY: HarperCollins Publishers, Inc.

Too Good to Leave, Too Bad to Stay. 1997. Mira Kirshenbaum. New York, NY: Penguin Books, USA, Inc.

Red Flags

How did we get into these painful relationships? What signs did we miss that would have tipped us off about our partner's serious emotional problems? We all know *now*, looking backwards, when the particular behaviors began to surface, but could we have seen the *tip of the iceberg* behavior sooner?

The following is a series of insights I've collected from various sources.

From narcissisticabuse@yahoogroups.com, a quote from a college professor:

> This is my favorite area of study in all of abnormal psychology. Why? There are two considerations: first, they are not psychotic, hallucinating, falling-down drunk or brain-damaged in most cases; they masquerade as normal humans. Second, they do not feel that anything is wrong with their attitudes or behavior, so they drive ordinary people crazy … they are *carriers* of stress so severe that it can led to a variety of Axis I diagnoses in loved ones. These people may be your mother, father, in-laws, nieces, nephews, aunts, cousins, friends, lovers, or neighbors. You have no idea that there is anything wrong, as long as you keep your distance psychologically. The instant that you become intimate with a person with one of the Personality Disorders, your reality will shift until you begin to wonder what is wrong with you.
>
> When I teach Personality Disorders, I think of it as a public service announcement – "This is what a person with XXX Personality Disorder is like; if your fiancé acts like this, give the ring back."
>
> People with Personality Disorders sometimes decompensate and are eligible for an Axis I diagnosis such as anxiety disorder, mood disorder, alcoholism, or sexual deviation.
>
> It is unlikely that a person with purely Axis II disorder will ever present for diagnosis or therapy on his own. This person is brought into therapy by the courts, a spouse, or employer unless he or she decompensates so badly that the person seeks out treatment for an Axis I disorder that is causing fairly extreme anguish.

All of the Personality Disorders have a quality of selfishness that you would expect in a child of about five or six; this means that a person with this type of disorder cannot have a reciprocal relationship with an adult, even if their behavior looks selfless.

People with Personality Disorders also make the same mistakes over and over, so that with time, one can see that they resist learning from past experience; everything that happens to them is *not* their fault.

From *Narcissism Revisited* at http://malignantlove.tripod.com:

The following two lists are suggested by members of my support group and myself. We are *not* mental health professionals. We are just some people trying to help each other cope. We believe that we have identified some of the *early warning* signs that we missed in ourselves and our abusers. Note that the abuser can be male or female; the victim can also be either male or female. Not every behavior listed below will be exhibited by a single individual. However, you may want to question your relationship if you find that a large number of these behaviors appear in yourself or your partner.

Abuser's Behavior

- Jealous of time or resources you give others
- Gets angry if you spend "too much time" with friends, family or children
- Insists that it is "a bad time" to talk to family on the phone
- Feels that resources are "wasted" if given to children
- Gets angry if you do favors for other people or give them things
- Would rather throw something away than give it to someone else
- Is disinterested in or feels threatened by your personal desires or goals
- Finds your hobbies boring, pointless, unproductive, or a waste of time
- Is uncooperative about attending parties or events that interest you
- Picks a fight or creates a crisis just before an event that is important to you

- States or implies that your interests should not interfere with spending time with them
- Is rude or inconsiderate of others in a self-centered way
- Insists on discussing something with you while you are trying to read or watch television
- Expects you to be the one who answers the door or telephone
- Interrupts others while they are talking on a consistent basis
- Will not act to accommodate others' convenience or comfort; won't go outside to smoke; will not turn down TV or radio while others are talking
- Is unconcerned and unapologetic if their rude behavior is pointed out
- Does not respect your right to make your own decisions
- Insists that your decision "affects them" and therefore should be a "joint" decision
- Gets angry or hurt if you don't take their advice
- Criticizes or questions the wisdom of decisions that you make without their input
- Considers their own logic or intellect to be superior to all others
- Insists that their way is the "right way"
- Claims that their arguments are based on logic or sound evidence and that yours are not
- Places no value on decisions made based on feelings or intuition
- Believes that any opinion you have is invalid, illogical, hysterical, or selfish
- Is completely intolerant of any criticism of their own behavior
- Is confident that their employer and/or employees are all defective somehow
- Considers your friends to be idiots
- Extremely opinionated and critical of others
- Racist or sexist
- Dogmatic about behavior in others
- Unwilling to tolerate opinions that differ from their own
- Has double standards for behavior
- Is rude to your family
- Dislikes your family
- Has "trouble" at work
- Is chronically unemployed or changes jobs frequently
- Explains employment set-backs as some sort of victimization
- Believes that their boss treats them poorly

- Believes that their co-workers are working against them
- Disregards laws or social customs that interfere with their own goals or pleasure
- Sees no point in observing holidays or giving gifts
- Is disinterested in following family or religious customs
- Believes that people who work hard for a living are "suckers"
- Is scornful of the government or the "system"
- Uses illegal drugs
- Is very concerned about their public image
- Treats you better in public than in private
- Gets angry at you if they believe that you have somehow made them look bad to others
- Brags about you or your accomplishments to others, but never compliments you in private
- Attempts to make you jealous or insecure
- Threatens to leave you
- Hints or states that they have other lovers waiting on the side
- Compares you to previous lovers
- Admires strangers and compares you to them
- Tells you that no one will ever care about you the way they do
- Is jealous and suspicious
- Accuses you of infidelity
- Insists that friends of the opposite sex are trying to seduce you
- States or implies that you got a job offer or interview because of your appearance
- Doesn't want you to take part in an activity or outing because you might meet someone else there
- Rushes the relationship
- Pressures you to move in together
- Pressures you to have sex before you are ready
- Proposes marriage early in the relationship
- Does not respect your privacy
- Reads your diary or journal
- Opens your mail
- Manipulates others to achieve their goals
- Uses guilt trips
- Does things that are dishonest or illegal
- Attempts to coerce you into doing things that make you uncomfortable
- Threatens suicide or homicide if you don't cooperate with them
- Lectures you endlessly until you agree

- Is easily angered at others who interfere with their activities
- Engages in Road Rage
- Reactions are out of proportion to level of inconvenience
- Is intolerant of children or animals
- Will not get up to feed or change the baby
- Is unwilling to have pets or children because of the mess or inconvenience
- Shows preferential treatment between children (especially natural vs. stepchildren)
- Believes that children don't deserve the same level of treatment or support as adults
- Insists that *they* are the victim in the relationship
- Accuses you of being selfish, rude, self-centered, uncooperative, etc.
- Claims that you are the one undermining the relationship
- Accuses you of not loving them or not caring about them
- Threatens suicide or homicide if you leave them
- Lack of empathy
- Inability to put themselves in another's shoes
- Unwilling to provide comfort to others unless *blame* clearly lies elsewhere
- Makes minimal effort to care for others when sick or injured, while complaining about the inconvenience
- Cruel to animals
- Considers donations to charity a waste
- Unable to acknowledge or respond to pain in others that is not clearly visible
- Turns up TV when you have a headache
- Insists on spicy food when you have an upset stomach
- Expects you to help with chores when you are feeling sick
- Tears down your self-esteem and erodes your confidence
- Tone of voice unreasonably deriding or scornful for the situation
- Questions your ability to do simple things
- Asks you to make a decision and then rejects your decision, often asking you to decide over again
- Accuses you of being overly sensitive to criticism
- Calls you names
- Criticizes you openly
- Interferes with or attempts to control your career
- Pressures you to quit or change your job

- Thinks that your employer interferes with your marriage
- Thinks that your co-workers/employer/employees are defective somehow
- Attempts to resolve conflicts you have at work for you
- Seeks to "help you" with your career, and is upset if you don't cooperate
- Attempts to choose your job or work projects for you
- Punishes you or threatens to punish you for "misbehaving"
- Strands you somewhere
- Gives you the silent treatment
- Yells at you
- Lectures you
- Believes that a "discussion" about your relationship is more important than any other obligation or activity
- Makes you late to work or social activities because they want to discuss something
- Picks a fight with you at bedtime and then won't let you go to sleep for hours

Victim's Behavior

Watch out for these behaviors in yourself. Members of my support group believe that these are warning signs of low self-esteem and behaviors that set us up to be abused:

- Fear of failure and extreme insecurity about your own competence
- Try hard to conceal or downplay any mistakes you make
- Are afraid to be seen as stupid, lazy, or weak
- Feel that you are "supposed" to be able to handle a situation or task
- Fear that others will think less of you if you quit
- Believe that no excuse is good enough for a mistake you have made
- Willing to overlook other people's flaws or mistakes
- Believe everyone else but you is perfect and has a good reason for making a mistake
- Believe that you can help others "live up to their potential"
- Not trusting your own judgment
- Feel as though your opinion is not as *worthy* as someone else's
- Find a *logical* argument to disregard your inner voice or gut feeling

- Assume that criticism you receive from others is valid
- Need another person's input before you can make a decision
- Not feeling that you deserve to be treated well
- Are willing to go to great inconvenience and trouble to avoid causing someone else inconvenience
- Don't want to appear *demanding* or to be considered a *trouble maker*
- Assume that if someone treats you poorly, then you must have done something wrong
- Expect and accept criticism when you have completed a task
- Are unwilling to be disruptive to the relationship
- Avoid discussing issues that you fear will upset your partner
- Are unwilling to break off a bad relationship because you don't want to hurt your partner
- Secretly wish that your partner would die, move away, find someone else, or offer to leave the relationship
- Allow others to make most decisions
- Let someone else make all the decisions with no input or discussion from you
- Allow others to talk you into a decision you don't like
- Make a decision to please others rather than yourself
- Choose a course of action because you don't want to hurt a particular person's feelings
- Find it easier to go along with others' decisions rather than stand your ground
- Behave as though you agree with others, even when you don't *parrot* someone else's opinions or behaviors
- Keep quiet when you disagree with something
- Allow someone to think by your silence that you agree with them, even when you don't
- Think that the subject is not worth an argument
- Act to protect others at your own expense
- Won't break up with a significant other strictly to avoid hurting their feelings
- Avoid saying what you want or need to say because you don't want to hurt someone
- Accept blame that is not yours to protect someone else
- Giving up things that are important to you to please others
- Give up hobbies or activities that aren't shared or approved of. Give away or sell precious mementos because they "clutter up the place"

- Keep photos or mementos in storage, rather than display them, because your abuser doesn't like them
- Isolate yourself from all people other than your abuser
- Allow friendships with people your abuser dislikes to wither away
- Visit or call family less and less because your abuser dislikes them
- Spend less time with friends, family, or co-workers because it "takes too much time"
- Never go anywhere without your abuser
- Conceal your abuser's behavior from others
- Believe that others "wouldn't understand" why a situation or behavior is "justified"
- Are embarrassed that you allow yourself to be treated this way
- Have been asked or coerced by your abuser to not tell
- Are afraid of being accused of "making them look bad"
- Take responsibility for things that are not your responsibility
- Help resolve other people's conflicts by acting as mediator.
- Apologize for things that *other* people did
- Cover for people who are not handling their own responsibilities
- Accept more than your fair share of blame in a conflict
- Apologize just so that the fight will end, not because you think you did something wrong
- Fix, clean up, or conceal something done by someone else to avoid being accused of having done it
- Attracted to authority figures
- Attracted to the smart, self-confident, powerful people
- Attempt to prove your worth to above types of people
- Are thrilled if above people *bother* to notice you
- Assume that the advice of above people is sound

From *Character Disorder* by J. Kent Griffiths, DSW, who says, "We all have several of these traits on a bad day, but if you see a preponderance of these attributes in yourself or the person you're worried about, it may indicate what is called a personality disorder. We should work on overcoming these attributes and avoid people who possess many of them."

Dr. Griffiths' website is www.members.aol.com/dswgriff.

- Emotional immaturity. Behavior is not age appropriate.
- Self-centeredness. He comes first and foremost. Is insincere about real interest in other people.
- Little if any remorse for mistakes
- Poor judgment
- Unreliability, undependability, irresponsibility
- Inability to profit from experience – does not learn a lesson from making mistakes
- Inability to postpone immediate gratification – what he wants, he wants now. Impulsive and demanding
- Conflict with, or defiance of, authority
- Lack of appreciation for the consequences of his actions
- Tendency to project his own shortcomings on to the world about him – frequent blaming. Never at fault
- Little if any conscience
- Behavior develops little sense of direction – often uninfluenced by concepts of right and wrong
- Gives lip service to professed values and beliefs
- Often involved with illegal or unethical acts
- Shallow interpersonal skills – inability to experience and verbalize deep feelings and emotions. Often insensitive to the needs and feelings of others. Cannot identify with how others feel.
- Ability to put up a good *front* to impress and exploit others
- Low stress tolerance with explosive behavior
- Can *con* to get what he wants to meet his needs, often at the expense of others. The behavior is highly repetitious and many people are used.
- Sees others as pawns on the chess board. Maneuvers people around for his own purposes. When done with them, they are *checkmated* or rejected.
- Ready rationalization – rarely at a loss for words – twists conversation to divorce himself from responsibility
- When he is trapped, he just keeps talking or changes the subject, or gets angry.

- Incapable of maintaining genuine loyalties to any person, group, or code
- Chronic lying
- Does/did poorly in school with attendance, grades, attitudes, and relationships with teachers. Was in conflict with parents over school performance.
- *Chip on shoulder* attitude – cocky and arrogant
- Rebellious to parents' authority. Violates standards of the home frequently.
- Cancels commitments without sound reason or warning.
- Uses friends for money, transportation, favors, time, attention, etc.
- A taker – not a giver. Gives for show but expects something in return.
- Glimpses of integrity and emotion are seen – but short lived. Gives you hope he's changing, but returns soon to deviant behavior.
- Lives life of avoiding responsibility vs. getting the job done.
- Poor self-motivation – often described as lazy and listless. Lacks ambition. Not helpful with routine chores.
- Fun is the cornerstone of his life.
- Sexually curious or active. Places great importance on his sexual abilities. Female sexual partner often feels used and demanded of.
- Lacks well-defined values.
- Comes across initially as caring and understanding and reads others "like a book" because he makes his business knowing how to maneuver people.
- In a trust relationship, inevitably betrays and violates the commitments and gets blocked emotionally when gets too close to those he says he loves.
- Angry mood most of the time.
- Uses sex to control, cover his insecurity or make up after a fight.
- Has no concept of open sharing of ideas, feelings, emotions. Conversation goes per his direction. He has the last word always. He determines how, when, where we talk, and about what he wants to talk about.
- Can show real tenderness of feeling, then return to customary behaviors. Two (or more) vastly different sides to his personality are seen.
- Poor planner with time and activity
- Is very slow to forgive others. Hangs on to resentment.

- Excessively concerned with personal appearance; e.g., hair, weight, car he drives, clothes, having money to flash, career dreaming
- Seems to enjoy disturbing others. Likes to agitate and disrupt for no apparent reason.
- Feels entitled to the *good life* without working for it.
- He never seems to get enough of what he wants. He leaves others drained and confused.
- Others get upset when in his presence. There's a feeling of guardedness, caution, and suspicion that he creates in others.
- Moody – switches from nice guy to anger without much provocation.
- Poor work history – quitting, being fired, interpersonal conflicts
- Repeatedly fails to honor financial obligations. Does not pay the bills in a responsible and timely way.
- Unable to sustain a totally faithful relationship with loved one of the opposite sex.
- Flirtatious, overly friendly. Makes inappropriate sexual comments to/about other women.
- Seldom expresses appreciation. Again, is thinking of his needs vs. the needs of others.
- Grandiose. Convinced that he knows more than other people and is correct and right in almost all he says and does.
- Clueless as to how he comes across to others and to how he is viewed. Gets defensive when confronted with his behavior. Never his fault. May be apologetic and seem sincere, but soon repeats offensive behavior without appearing to have learned from it.
- Motive for behavior is usually self-serving, and he does not recognize it.
- Can get very emotional, even tearful, but behavior is more about show or frustration rather than contrition or sorrow.
- He breaks women's spirits to keep them dependent.
- Survives on threats, intimidations to keep others chained to him.
- Sabotages anything that makes his spouse/girlfriend happy. Wants her to be happy only through him and to have few/no outside interests/friends/family.
- Highly contradictory. He loves me, he hates me. He threatens me with poverty, then indulges me or our relationship.

- He is always working somebody over – either subtly or aggressively for a favor, deal, break, freebie, discount, etc.
- Double standard. He is free to do his thing, but expects others to be what he wants them to be/do. He doesn't let others be themselves.
- Convincing. Successful at getting other people to believe in his perception of a problem. Is adamant that people side with him vs. allowing them to feel/believe differently.
- Hides who he really is from everyone. No one really knows the real him.
- Scorns everyone/everything that he disagrees with. Does not allow for differences to be respected. Scorns the responsible world.
- Difficult to pin him down to a certain level of integrity that you can live with. Resists all efforts to define his values, behaviors, standards.
- Kind to you usually only if he's getting from you what he wants.
- He has to be right. He has to win. He has to look good.
- He announces, not discusses. He tells, not asks.
- He does not discuss openly beforehand. You get to deal with *after the fact* information.
- Controls money of others but spends freely on himself and others.
- You end up feeling responsible for the problem. He gets to your feelings. No matter what, he wins, you lose.
- He wins at the expense of your feelings. Thinks only of the end result without considering your feelings or needs in the process.
- Attitude of "I'll meet your needs if you meet mine. If you don't, I'll find someone else who will or I will not meet yours."
- Unilateral condition of, "I'm OK and justified, so I don't need to hear your position or ideas."
- Does not take responsibility for his behavior.
- The hurt he describes is because he got caught, or he's mad that you're mad, and not because he believes he made a mistake.
- Secret life. You're often wondering what he does or who he is that you don't know about.
- Always feels misunderstood.
- Most of the time you feel miserable living with this person. When it's good, you relish the peace, but that is usually short lived.

- He is so skilled at making a mountain out of a molehill, and you become so tired of the conflict. It drains all of your energy, love and hope.
- Is usually through listening once he's made his arguments.
- We talk about his feelings, not mine.
- Unchallenged by people because they seem to be put off by him, afraid of him, or he eludes them.
- Is not interested in problem-solving openly.
- Seems very interested in discerning personalities, so that he can strategize how to manipulate them.

~ ~ ~

And finally, Dear Abby chimes in with her list of signs to tip us off to a potential abuser:

DEAR ABBY: The letter from "At My Wit's End," whose best friend's husband was insanely jealous, prompted me to write.

For 13 years, I was married to a very controlling, much older man. A woman named "Helen" from church would call me occasionally. Since I wasn't allowed to have friends, each time she called, my husband would make a scene in the background. I was extremely embarrassed, but one day, she said: "He's trying to run me off. He may have been in your life a long time before me, but I'll be around long after he's gone!"

That statement caused me to review my situation and realize the extent to which I was being controlled. Suddenly, I experienced a feeling of power where before I felt helpless. I came to realize that I was miserable in my marriage, but I had believed it was all my fault. Had it not been for Helen's comment, I might still be in that abusive relationship (which it was).

That was 20 years ago. I divorced him, and my life has changed tremendously since then. Please, Abby, tell "Wit's End" she may be her friend's only link to a new life.

– Been There in Texas

DEAR BEEN THERE: I'll do better than that. I'll point out that being isolated from friends and family by a partner – male or female – is one sign of a potential abuser. Read on for some other signs (adapted with permission from the Project for Victims of Family Violence in Fayetteville, Ark.), any one of which could be a sign of abuse.

- PUSHES FOR QUICK INVOLVEMENT: Comes on strong, claiming, "I've never felt loved like this by anyone." An abuser pressures the new partner for an exclusive commitment almost immediately.
- JEALOUS: Excessively possessive; calls constantly or visits unexpectedly; prevents you from going to work because "you might meet someone"; checks the mileage on your car.
- CONTROLLING: Interrogates you intensely (especially if you're late) about whom you talked to and where you were; keeps all the money; insists you ask permission to go anywhere or do anything.
- UNREALISTIC EXPECTATIONS: Expects you to be the perfect mate and meet his or her every need.
- ISOLATION: Tries to cut you off from family and friends; accuses people who are your supporters of "causing trouble." The abuser may deprive you of a phone or car, or try to prevent you from holding a job.
- BLAMES OTHERS FOR PROBLEMS OR MISTAKES: It's always someone else's fault if something goes wrong.
- MAKES OTHERS RESPONSIBLE FOR HIS OR HER FEELINGS: The abuser says, "You make me angry," instead of, "I am angry," or says, "You're hurting me by not doing what I tell you."
- HYPERSENSITIVITY: Is easily insulted, claiming hurt feelings when he or she is really mad. Rants about the injustice of things that are just a part of life.
- CRUELTY TO ANIMALS AND CHILDREN: Kills or punishes animals brutally. Also, may expect children to do things that are far beyond their ability (whips a three-year-old for wetting a diaper), or may tease them until they cry. Sixty-five per cent of abusers who beat their partner will also abuse children.
- "PLAYFUL" USE OF FORCE DURING SEX: Enjoys throwing you down or holding you down against your will during sex; finds the idea of rape exciting.
- VERBAL ABUSE: Constantly criticizes or says blatantly cruel, hurtful things; degrades, curses, calls you ugly names. This may also involve sleep deprivation, waking you up with relentless verbal abuse.
- RIGID SEX ROLES: Expects you to serve, obey, stay at home.
- SUDDEN MOOD SWINGS: Switches from sweet to violent in minutes.
- PAST BATTERING: Admits to hitting a mate in the past, but says the person "made" him (or her) do it.

- THREATS OF VIOLENCE: Says things like, "I'll break your neck," or "I'll kill you," and then dismisses them with, "Everybody talks that way," or "I didn't really mean it." If the abuse has gone this far – it's time to get help or get out!

Guidelines for Leaving a BPD Relationship

A Guide to Leaving a Partner with Borderline Personality Disorder, written by Hal Broome, a member of the Land of Oz online support group for partners of those with borderline personality disorder (LandofOz @yahoogroups.com).

Perhaps as many as 10 – 14 per cent of the general population suffer from Borderline Personality Disorder (BPD), with research suggesting even larger percentages for the gay and lesbian communities. Despite the great numbers of people suffering from the disorder, and the sometimes serious effect of its presence upon the partners of people with BPD, there is little information available for those partners in handling the mental and physical abuse that may occur because of the disorder.. This document itself will not address those issues; rather, it is a quick guide intended to cover the possible consequences of leaving a partner with BPD, with collective pointers from people who have gone through the experience themselves.

This is necessary, as many of the traits of BPD are distinctly antagonistic to peaceful settlements or simple partings. If your troubled partner displays any of the following characteristics, you may be dealing with BPD and need to know how its traits have a particular impact on your relationship:

The person with a borderline personality is impulsive in areas that have a potential for self-destruction. Relationships with others are intense and unstable. The person will go through frantic efforts to avoid real or imagined abandonment by others, and express mood instability and inappropriate anger. There may also be identity uncertainty concerning self-image, long-term goals or career choice, sexual orientation, choice of friends, and values.

People with this disorder tend to see things in terms of extremes, either all good or all bad. They view themselves as victims of circumstances and take little responsibility for themselves or for their problems.

Symptoms of BPD include:

- Unstable interpersonal relationships
- Frequent displays of temper
- Inappropriate anger
- Recurrent suicide gestures
- Feelings of emptiness and boredom

- Intolerance of being alone
- Impulsiveness in at least two of the following areas: money, substance abuse, sexual relationships, reckless driving, binge eating, shoplifting.

From Yahoo! Health Guide; www.yahoo.com and search for "borderline personality disorder"

You may have come across this document because you already know or suspect BPD in your partner. Do not attempt to diagnose them, but be aware that if you recognize any of the above traits, or already know the diagnosis of BPD, then you should cautiously assume that all these traits, even ones you have not yet seen, may co-exist, impeding or endangering your attempt to leave the relationship. The following guide assumes a "worst case" scenario, but, as with any human disorder, there are obviously individual variations, with some of the characteristics more prominent and others less so. Let your instincts and knowledge of your partner be your guide, but be prepared to deal with traits that you have not yet witnessed.

To leave or Not to Leave:

This document cannot decide for you whether you should leave or not. Instead, it is aimed at those who have already decided to leave, and aims to cover the possible pitfalls involved, with suggestions to ease your way out of the relationship with a minimum of fuss and a maximum of safety.

Even if you have decided to leave, you may still find yourself beforehand grappling with counter-reasons to stay. Some of the more common are listed below:

- HOPE that things will be "the way it used to be." BPD mood swings may have conditioned you to think that, after a bad period, things will get better. However, if you recognize such a clear cycle, be aware they may also get worse again! In some cases, there may not be another swing to "the way it used to be," and the behavior or abuse may worsen.
- UNCLEAR THINKING. People in an abusive relationship may be under not only stress but also shock, and so may not think clearly. They may find themselves confused over the way the partner with BPD alternates between awful rages and then normal, loving behavior. Keep in contact with friends, and listen

closely to their comments; they may have a clearer view of the person and relationship than you do. If you are disturbed or confused by your partner's behavior, seek therapy to help in coping with its unpredictable nature.

- EXHAUSTION. Dealing daily with the fear of a rage, or constantly being on guard against other strange behaviors, will leave you exhausted to the point you may not want to do ANYTHING, let alone pack up and get out of the relationship. If you can, find some time alone to rest and think about your situation from a distance.
- SUBSTANCE ABUSE. If, in your stressed state, you are indulging in substance abuse to "cope," do your best to taper off or quit entirely – you need to be clear- headed not only for your partner's benefit, but your own.
- LONELINESS. Some fear that all they have is their partner. Out of their fears of abandonment, the BPD partner may have been pushing others away from you, and you may have been giving too much attention to the relationship as a way of avoiding conflict. Your own dependency issues may be at work as well. Keep in contact with friends and family, and seek therapy if you are feeling isolated.
- STAYING TO HELP. You might want to stay to help; but, as in alcoholism, your BPD partner cannot get better until *they* want to do so. Getting help is *their* decision, not yours. Your primary responsibility is to yourself. If you want your partner in therapy, the best course is to set an example and get therapy for *yourself.* Be aware that even the act of getting therapy for yourself might disturb your partner and consequently, their behavior might worsen, so don't overplay the fact that you are seeking help.
- KEEP IN MIND: *You* are a trigger of the disorder! That is the nature of BPD. Rather than making the situation worse, it might help *both* of you if you leave. Certainly, your presence might inadvertently be making the BPD person worse, as people with BPD tend to relive earlier traumas through their significant others, alternating between paradoxical feelings of extreme engulfment or extreme isolation. You did not deliberately cause these feelings, but your presence may be exacerbating the BPD's response. You may also find that a partner with BPD may leave *you* suddenly, and for no apparent reason, due to the stress of alternating feelings of "too much closeness" and fear of abandonment.

- FEAR that the partner might commit suicide if you leave. You are not responsible for another person's actions. Some people with BPD use the threat of suicide to prevent their biggest fear: abandonment. But while threatening suicide, they may also be making long-term arrangements, having affairs to replace you, even, as one woman found, pocketing away common money for the impending divorce. However, if a threat is actually attempted, do not hesitate to bring in not only medical personnel, but police. You cannot shoulder on yourself the responsibilities of doctors and legal authorities. If the partner is in therapy, alert the therapist to any suggestion of suicide.
- FEAR that your partner may hurt themselves in other ways. A well-known BPD trait is "self-mutilation," whereby the distressed person cuts or otherwise mutilates their own body in an effort to escape inner pain. Always alert your partner's doctor or therapist if you see this happening, or even if it is merely threatened.

Even if you stay undecided about leaving, always have a "sudden exit strategy" in place. Have a packed suitcase, spare money, essential items in one place, and a safe residence to go to on a moment's notice. Do not tolerate physical abuse or even the threat of it; leave immediately. When a BPD partner is raging, they are not thinking clearly, and you should definitely leave the situation, if only temporarily, until the partner calms down. If you make a habit of this, they will also be less suspicious when it is time to make your final departure.

Before leaving:

The best way to leave a partner with BPD is through careful planning. Once you have made the decision to leave, you should take the following steps before you leave:

Keep the "sudden exit strategy" in place and even start adding to it with more details. You do not ideally want to leave on the spur of the moment, but keep in mind that people with BPD fear abandonment, and therefore may worsen their behavior if any whiff of your intention to leave is detected. "If in doubt – get out!" Pack needed items a few at a time beforehand, to not only be prepared but also to delay suspicions from your partner.

Consult a therapist about your situation. Therapy will help you deal with the emotional abuse characteristic of relationships with BPD, and provide a safe and assuring environment in which to talk over your feelings about the partner. You may also learn ways of coping and re-acting to the disorder that shield both you and your partner. Question the therapist beforehand about their knowledge of BPD; the disorder is not so widely known that you can assume they are familiar with its particular issues.

If your partner is in therapy, tell their therapist about your intention of leaving. An ethical therapist will NOT tell your partner of your in-tent, but can help prepare them for the event, easing not only your departure, but also your ex-partner's reaction to the change.

Consult a lawyer. There are many legal ramifications of leaving your own home, or forcing an abusive partner to leave a shared home. If you are not legally married, you may not have the normal court protec-tions. Lawyers are also useful in discussing such issues as possible re-straining orders. If you are planning divorce, it is very important that you make legal moves carefully before you make your intentions known to your partner. There is also the possibility of counter-lawsuits from the abandoned party against which you may have to defend yourself. Since laws vary from state to state, and country to country, and you may find conflicting advice from friends and family over these laws, give full weight to your lawyer's advice.

Document as fully as you can the abusive actions of your partner! Keep a diary of strange behavior. This will be valuable evidence in case authorities "do not believe you" or if the person with BPD makes false accusations or blames you for the breakup. Given that BPD behavior is more commonly witnessed by the partner, while the person with BPD may act normally in front of others, you may need backup to your claims of abusive behaviors, as others may not believe you. You may also find that referring to your documentation strengthens your resolve to leave.

Due to the sometimes extreme reactions of BPD behavior, it is wise to plan to *take all of your personal possessions with you when you leave*. You do not want to be "held hostage" to personal items that you may want to retrieve later; you may even find them missing or de-stroyed. Once again, consult a lawyer over the legal ramifications of abandoning or taking mutual property. Instead of taking everything at once, you may decide to move individual items one at a time, espe-cially personal items, or those useful in an independent living situation or "sudden exit." Be careful, however, not to tip off your partner of your intention of leaving by removing everything at once, or obvious items that suggest you are leaving.

Do not prematurely tell the person with BPD that you are leaving! It will backfire as a threat, due, once again, to the sometimes extreme reactions of the disorder. So when leaving, do it suddenly, previously unannounced, and, preferably, in the presence of *strangers*. Because people with BPD tend to "act out" their disorder more around people they know, you will be inhibiting that behavior by having strangers around you. Friends may volunteer their help, but you are better off paying for a moving company to aid you – this not only makes the move happen quickly, it also furnishes strangers who can witness any bad reactions. A BPD person caught off-guard, in the presence of strangers, and during a sudden, quickly-occurring move, is safer than a BPD person who has had time to prepare their response!

If your household has guns, remove them to a safe and secret place right before you start moving/leaving.

Let both your workplace *and* the police know about your impending departure ahead of time. As abandoned BPDs may start a "smear" campaign against you – they may even call the police on *you* – this helps to short-circuit that attempt. Have your documentation of the abusive behavior at hand. Police may be puzzled why you are still in the abusive situation, and think you simply need an escort back to the premises to pick up your stuff, so make them very aware that the real danger with BPD is not so much in the staying, but the act of leaving! Have them arrive shortly before the movers to either witness as strangers, or to talk to the BPD partner and warn them about doing anything rash. Remember, as a taxpayer, you have the right to ask for a police escort at any time.

Avoid giving the BPD partner *any* reason not to trust you. If they are having an affair, *do not* have an affair yourself, as you may find the reaction much greater than you anticipated (especially from one who is indulging in the same behavior). Likewise, you may find any distrust of you turned into material for a "smear" campaign as listed above.

Due to the nature of BPD, you may be "hoovered" at the time of leaving or afterwards. This means your partner will suddenly be on their best behavior in an attempt to suck you back into the relationship. Keep in mind the cycle of their behavior; even when things return to "good," they will also return to "bad," and the fear of abandonment may make the "bad" even worse when it returns! To guard against the "hoover," you may want to *not* leave a forwarding address or phone number. If you *must* do so, leave the number of a "neutral" third party, such as your lawyer or a mutual friend who can screen what is a reasonable and what is an abusive request.

Concentrate on the "right now." Instead of letting all the preparation overwhelm you, make a list, and follow it one step at a time. Unless there is the real threat of physical violence, you have all the time you need to prepare.

Always be aware that the time shortly before and after leaving may be the most dangerous period of all. As people with BPD are very sensitive to being abandoned, they may increase their strange or abusive behavior beforehand or afterwards, and even exhibit symptoms you have not yet seen, such as suicidal gestures or threats against your person or belongings.

As you leave:

These are specific actions or items to consider or do as you move out:

Once again, take everything you rightfully own with you. Even if the person with BPD expresses a desire for you to leave, they may still latch upon your remaining possessions as a "hostage" in an attempt to keep you in contact. Or, they may rage against the departure and destroy or throw away any item that reminds them of you. Since some people with BPD have trouble "remembering how they feel" about other people, they may show a strong unwillingness to part with items that remind them of their partner.

Even people with BPD who want you to leave may be tense or, possibly, temporarily psychotic as you pack. If you can, pack and move when they are not present. If you are unsure whether they will be present or not, have strangers on hand as a means of keeping the BPD in check (people with BPD who cannot control their rages in front of you may sometimes show remarkable restraint in the presence of strangers). Once again, as a citizen, you have the right to request a police escort in or out of a potentially abusive situation – use it!

Do not linger after packing or make much of your going. This may only increase the stress of the BPD partner and thereby cause a rage or short psychotic episode. It will not do your stress any good either.

As noted before, you may want to avoid leaving your new address or even phone number behind with the BPD partner. This lessens the chance of their playing upon your own ambivalence about the move and courting you back into the abusive relationship, or of venting their anger on you later. If you must stay in contact, call them from a safe place, or leave a third party's phone number behind as the mediator.

After you leave:

It is best to have absolutely *no contact* afterwards; if, again, you must because of obligations (children, divorce, common property to divide), wait until such time as you feel not only comfortable, but also *resolved* not to continue the relationship. Do not meet alone, either, if you must, but have an outside observer, preferably a stranger to the BPD, on hand.

Those with shared children may still need to maintain some contact. In this situation, keep the conversations strictly on the topic of the children, and if the former partner starts getting personal about your relationship, cut the conversation short. The same advice goes for e-mail; if it gets personal, send a short, concise message back, then delete the offending e-mail. Send unofficial postal letters back, "return to sender," and unopened. Or, if your attorney has asked you for documentation, you might consider forwarding all mail unopened to your attorney.

Mourn the relationship but don't wallow in it; focus on some outside target/task to be accomplished that has nothing to do with the ex-partner. If you have left your home to get away from the BPD, you will find plenty to do! Settling in elsewhere, making new friends, telling family members and others about your transition, etc., are all worthy goals to occupy your attention.

Be aware that things don't magically "get better" the moment you are out the door. Some common experiences related afterwards by people who have left a person with BPD include:

- *PTSD.* A period of time in which a lot of the anxiety and tension from the experience will well up and seemingly overwhelm you. You may be experiencing post traumatic stress disorder (PTSD), or you may simply find that you have been "hyper-vigilant" for so long that it is almost a habit! Be aware that these feelings will slowly subside; continue therapy if possible. Expect to feel exhausted; take care of yourself and rest.
- *Disturbed Dreams.* A healthy person processes events through their dreaming; so your dreams may continue to be about the situation/BPD person for some time. These dreams may go away, only to crop up much later. Know that this is normal; use dreams as useful tools to analyze your reaction to the stressful events that triggered them. You may even gauge your progress by how the bad dreams are fading.

- *Feelings of Doubt.* Did you do the right thing? How is that person with BPD doing? Am I BPD, too? Remember that you may have acquired such BPD traits as projection by merely being in contact with the disorder; a therapist will help you straighten out any feelings of doubt about these issues. Your partner functioned without you before you met them – as did you! – so concentrate on your own needs and priorities.
- *Loneliness.* You may find yourself feeling isolated in your new surroundings and without a support group. You may feel that you do not have the energy left to make new friends, or even to confront old ones. You may not want to go anywhere; you may feel depressed. So treat yourself: go for a walk. Go to a coffee shop and be open to conversation. If you have hobbies, like painting, writing, reading, etc., use this new-found time – when you are no longer dealing constantly with BPD issues – to pursue your interests. Go back to school. Look upon this as a new beginning!
- You will also find during this period that having your familiar things around you helps. So pay close attention to the advice about 'TAKE EVERYTHING YOU OWN WITH YOU!' Conversely, don't let loneliness drive you into a new relationship quickly, at least not until you have gone through a healthy period of self-examination. "Why" did you get into that relationship in the first place? This is a good time to examine your family background and see what blinded you to the fact that the BPD person was trouble (it is true that people with BPD are sometimes very good at hiding their disorder, but in retrospect, you will see that some early signs were there). You may have doubts or fears about making new friends or dating because you are afraid that you will once again choose a BPD partner. Keep in mind that you are now an expert on recognizing BPD symptoms, and so practice looking for these signs and deciding if your fears are real or not. Continue therapy. Self-awareness is actually one of the "gifts" received from having been in an abusive situation; with enough work, you may actually come out of the experience as a stronger person. Be warned again, however, about rushing into any new relationships before you have fully processed the previous bad one!
- *Encountering the 'Smear' Campaign.* If your partner degraded previous partners, you may rest assured they are probably "bad-mouthing" you. Remember what kindergarten taught you: sticks

and stones may break your bones, but words will never hurt you! Put yourself above blame, be an adult and get on with your life. Of course, some smears can get ugly: lawsuits and nasty divorce proceedings sometimes occur as yet another means to keep you from "abandoning" the person with BPD. An abandoned BPD partner may try retaliating as "punishment." This can be avoided or ameliorated somewhat by paying careful attention to the "Before You Leave" section; anticipate how you may be smeared and 'nip it in the bud' before you leave. Also, it is harder to smear someone who is no longer there to be smeared! Keep the "no contact" rule. And, once again, *never* give the person with BPD reasons not to trust you, either before or after you leave!

* *Forgiveness.* While it is easy to be mad at either the person with BPD or the disorder itself and its effect on you, personal recovery from the experience is greatly facilitated by forgiveness and understanding on your part. Find out as much as you can about BPD: this will help you to forgive the person suffering from the disorder (as their actions are signs of their own suffering, and have little or nothing to do with you personally). This also gives you a better "feel" for recognizing the symptoms if you encounter them in other people, and, in turn, will increase your social confidence.

So, having faced all of the above, how long does it take to really recover from an abusive BPD relationship? Count on the first three months or so to be the worst, when the dreams, anxiety, new surroundings, doubts, exhaustion, etc., are all on the forefront. But if you keep to "one issue at a time" and don't allow yourself to be overwhelmed, you will find your tensions easing slowly but surely. After a year or two of steady self-care, you may be amazed that you even allowed yourself to fall into such a relationship – and even more amazed to find that you now have the inner strength and awareness to avoid it in the future!

Domestic Violence: Safety Plan Guidelines

© 2004 by the National Center for Victims of Crime (www.ncvc.org)

These safety suggestions have been compiled from safety plans distributed by state domestic violence coalitions from around the country. Following these suggestions is not a guarantee of safety, but could help to improve your safety situation.

Personal Safety with an Abuser:

- Identify your partner's use and level of force so that you can assess danger to you and your children before it occurs.
- Try to avoid an abusive situation by leaving.
- Identify safe areas of the house where there are no weapons and where there are always ways to escape. If arguments occur, try to move to those areas.
- Don't run to where the children are, as your partner may hurt them as well.
- If violence is unavoidable, make yourself a small target; dive into a corner and curl up into a ball with your face protected and arms around each side of your head; fingers entwined.
- If possible, have a phone accessible at all times and know the numbers to call for help. Know where the nearest pay phone is located. Know your local battered women's shelter number. Don't be afraid to call the police.
- Let trusted friends and neighbors know of your situation and develop a plan and visual signal for when you need help.
- Teach your children how to get help. Instruct them not to get involved in the violence between you and your partner. Plan a code word to signal to them that they should get help or leave the house.
- Tell your children that violence is never right, even when someone they love is being violent. Tell them that neither you nor they are at fault or cause the violence, and that when anyone is being violent, it is important to keep safe.
- Practice how to get out safely. Practice with your children.
- Plan for what you will do if your children tell your partner of your plan or if your partner otherwise finds out about your plan.
- Keep weapons like guns and knives locked up and as inaccessible as possible.
- Make a habit of backing the car into the driveway and keeping it fueled.

- Keep the driver's door unlocked and others locked – for a quick escape.
- Try not to wear scarves or long jewelry that could be used to strangle you.
- Create several plausible reasons for leaving the house at different times of the day or night. Call a domestic violence hotline periodically to assess your options and get a supportive, understanding ear.

Getting Ready to Leave:

- Keep any evidence of physical abuse, such as pictures, etc.
- Know where you can go to get help; tell someone what is happening to you.
- If you are injured, go to a doctor or an emergency room and report what happened to you. Ask that they document your visit.
- Plan with your children and identify a safe place for them (for example, a room with a lock or a friend's house where they can go for help). Reassure them that their job is to stay safe, not to protect you.
- Contact your local battered women's shelter and find out about laws and other resources available to you before you have to use them during a crisis.
- Keep a journal of all violent incidences, noting dates, events and threats made, if possible.
- Acquire job skills as you can, such as learning to type or taking courses at a community college.
- Try to set money aside or ask friends or family members to hold money for you.
- Store some belongings with a friend or relative. Leave clothing, medications, your Social Security card, a credit card (if possible), citizenship documents, children's school/medical records, children's toys, insurance information, copies of birth certificates, money and other valued personal possessions with them.

The Day You Leave:

- Leave when it is least expected – for example during times of agreement and calm.
- Create a false trail. Call motels, real estate agencies, schools in a town at least six hours away from where you plan to relocate.

Ask questions that require a call back to your house in order to leave those phone numbers on record.

- Request a police escort. If your abuser will be present when you leave, you may want to contact your police department so an officer is standing by, protecting you.

General Guidelines for Leaving an Abusive Relationship:

- If you need to sneak away, be prepared.
- Make a plan for how and where you will escape.
- Plan for a quick escape.
- Put aside emergency money as you can.
- Hide an extra set of car keys.
- Pack an extra set of clothes for yourself and your children and store them at a trusted friend or neighbor's house. Try to avoid using next-door neighbors, close family members and mutual friends.
- Take with you important phone numbers of friends, relatives, doctors, schools, etc., as well as other important items, including:
  - Driver's license
  - Regularly needed medication
  - List of credit cards held by self or jointly or the credit cards themselves if you have access to them
  - Pay stubs, checkbooks and information about bank accounts and other assets
- If time is available, also take:
  - Citizenship documents (such as your passport, Green Card, etc.)
  - Titles, deeds, and other property information
  - Medical records
  - Children's school and immunization records
  - Insurance information
  - Copy of marriage license, birth certificates, will, and other legal documents
  - Verification of social security numbers
  - Welfare identification
  - Valued pictures, jewelry, or personal possessions

After Leaving the Abusive Relationship:

If getting a restraining order and the offender is leaving:

- Change locks and phone number.
- Change work hours and route taken to work.
- Change route taken to transport children to school.
- Keep a certified copy of your restraining order with you at all times.
- Inform friends, neighbors and employers that you have a restraining order in effect.
- Give copies of restraining order to employers, neighbors, and schools along with a picture of the offender.
- Call law enforcement to enforce the order.

If you leave:

- Consider renting a post office box or using the address of a friend for your mail.
- Be aware that addresses are on restraining orders and police reports.
- Be careful to whom you give your new address and phone number.
- Change your work hours if possible.
- Alert school authorities of situation.
- Consider changing your children's schools.
- Reschedule appointments that offender is aware of.
- Use different stores and frequent different social spots.
- Alert neighbors and request that they call the police if they feel you may be in danger.
- Talk to trusted people about the violence.
- Replace wooden doors with steel or metal doors.
- Install security systems if possible.
- Install a motion-sensitive lighting system that lights up when a person approaches the home.
- Tell people you work with about the situation and have your calls screened by one receptionist if possible.
- Tell people who take care of your children which individuals are allowed to pick up your children. Explain your situation to them and provide them with a copy of the restraining order.
- Call the telephone company to request caller ID. Ask that your phone be blocked so that if you call, neither your partner nor anyone else will be able to get your new, unlisted phone number.

THE WORLD OF
THE BPD'S PARTNER

POT-SHOTS NO. 1250.

A TERRIBLE THING HAS HAPPENED ~

I'VE LOST
MY WILL
TO SUFFER.

Ashleigh
Brilliant·com

©BRILLIANT ENTERPRISES 1977.

POT-SHOTS NO. 1363.

SOME OF
THE STRANGEST
PEOPLE
IN THE
WORLD

ARE

MARRIED TO EACH OTHER.

Ashleigh
Brilliant·com

©BRILLIANT ENTERPRISES 1977.

POT-SHOTS NO. 1275.

SOMETHING
MUST
BE WRONG
IF I GET
HOMESICK
EVEN WHEN
I'M AT HOME.

©BRILLIANT ENTERPRISES 1977.

Ashleigh
Brilliant·com

POT-SHOTS NO. 1145.

THE SHOW MUST GO ON

BUT
I DON'T HAVE TO
STAY AND WATCH!

Ashleigh
Brilliant.com

©BRILLIANT ENTERPRISES 1977.

POT-SHOTS NO. 1213.

COMMUNICATION
WITH THE DEAD
IS ONLY A LITTLE
MORE DIFFICULT
THAN
COMMUNICATION
WITH
SOME OF
THE LIVING.

©BRILLIANT ENTERPRISES 1977. Ashleigh Brilliant.com

POT-SHOTS NO. 803.

I'LL BE GLAD WHEN IT'S ALL OVER,

AND I CAN TAKE MY SMILE OFF.

POT-SHOTS NO. 1726.

UNLESS YOU MOVE,

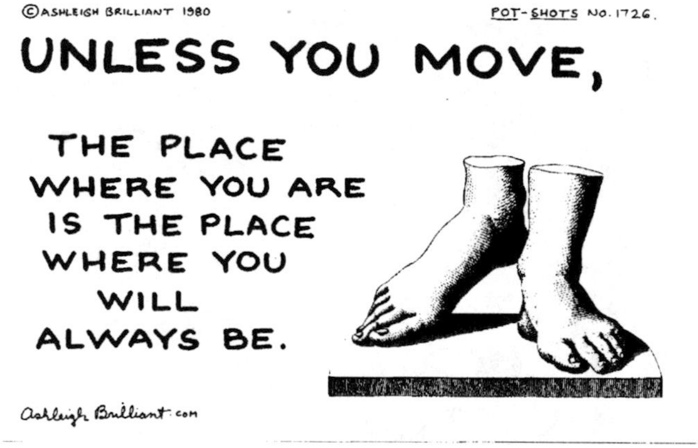

THE PLACE
WHERE YOU ARE
IS THE PLACE
WHERE YOU
WILL
ALWAYS BE.

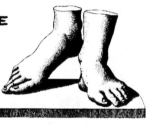

Ashleigh Brilliant.com

POT-SHOTS NO. 1457.

I'LL BE GLAD
TO DISCUSS
THE PROBLEM,

AS SOON AS
YOU REMOVE
YOUR HANDS
FROM MY THROAT.

Ashleigh Brilliant · com

SUDDENLY
I LOST
ALL CONTROL
OF MYSELF,

AND STARTED
MISSING
YOU.

POT-
SHOTS
NO. 1984.

©ASHLEIGH BRILLIANT 1980.

©BRILLIANT ENTERPRISES 1975.

POT-SHOTS NO. 817.

YOU KNOW I'LL ALWAYS
STAY WITH YOU,

UNTIL I CAN'T
BEAR IT
ANY LONGER.

© ASHLEIGH BRILLIANT 1981.   POT-SHOTS NO. 2076.

WILL ALL THOSE
WHO FEEL POWERLESS
TO INFLUENCE EVENTS

PLEASE SIGNIFY
BY
MAINTAINING
THEIR USUAL
SILENCE.

Ashleigh Brilliant
.COM

© BRILLIANT ENTERPRISES 1974.   POT- SHOTS NO. 649

I WISH THEY'D PASS
MORE LAWS

TO
PROTECT ME
FROM MYSELF.

Ashleigh
Brilliant.com

© BRILLIANT ENTERPRISES 1975.   POT- SHOTS NO. 762.

I'M SO GLAD
I HAVE YOU
TO
ESCAPE
FROM.

Ashleigh Brilliant.com

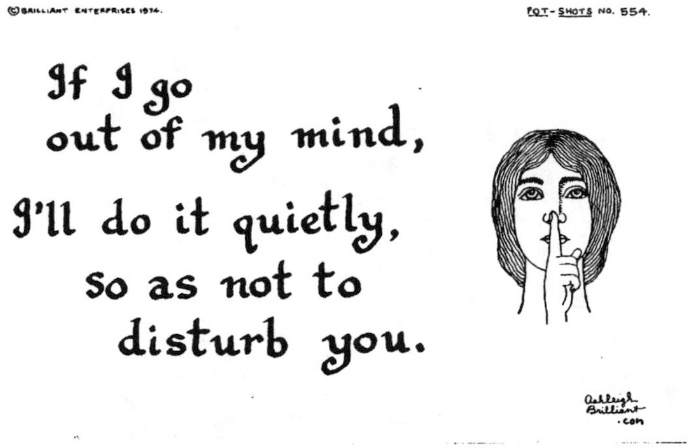

© BRILLIANT ENTERPRISES 1974.   POT-SHOTS NO. 554.

If I go
out of my mind,
I'll do it quietly,
so as not to
disturb you.

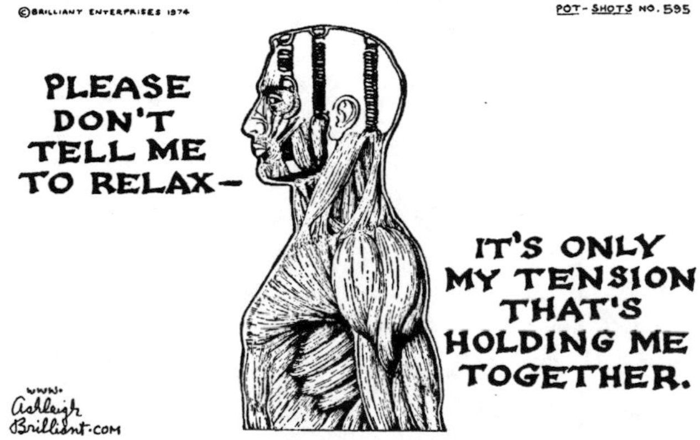

© BRILLIANT ENTERPRISES 1974   POT-SHOTS NO. 595

PLEASE
DON'T
TELL ME
TO RELAX—

IT'S ONLY
MY TENSION
THAT'S
HOLDING ME
TOGETHER.

© BRILLIANT ENTERPRISES 1974.   POT-SHOTS NO. 602

LET'S STAY
TOGETHER

AND DRAG
EACH OTHER
DOWN.

POT-SHOTS NO. 473

NORMAL TIMES MAY POSSIBLY BE OVER FOREVER!

Ashleigh Brilliant .com

POT-SHOTS NO. 2126.

Ashleigh Brilliant .com

IF
YOU HIDE
YOUR
REAL FEELINGS
FOR
LONG ENOUGH,
YOU MAY
EVENTUALLY
FORGET
WHAT THEY ARE.

© BRILLIANT ENTERPRISES 1973

POT ~ SHOTS NO. 446

Until recently,
I thought I was
someone I knew.

Ashleigh
Brilliant
·com

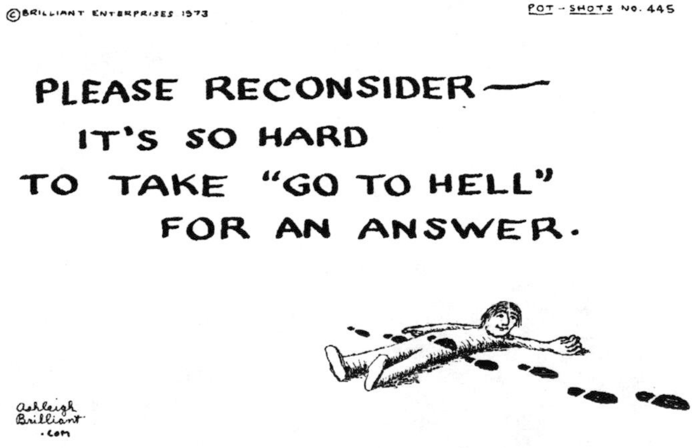

© BRILLIANT ENTERPRISES 1973

POT ~ SHOTS NO. 445

PLEASE RECONSIDER —
IT'S SO HARD
TO TAKE "GO TO HELL"
FOR AN ANSWER.

Ashleigh
Brilliant·
·com

© BRILLIANT ENTERPRISES 1973

POT ~ SHOTS NO. 451

YOU KNOW
I'LL ALWAYS HELP YOU
IF YOU NEED ME

SO PLEASE,
DON'T NEED ME.

Ashleigh
Brilliant · COM

©ASHLEIGH BRILLIANT 1981.

POT-SHOTS NO. 2252.

THE BEST THING ABOUT MY LACK OF PROGRESS

IS THAT I CAN'T FALL BACK VERY FAR.

Ashleigh
Brilliant.com

©ASHLEIGH
BRILLIANT
1981.

POT-SHOTS NO. 2276.

I'M NOT YET DESPERATE ENOUGH TO DO ANYTHING ABOUT THE CONDITIONS WHICH ARE DRIVING ME TO DESPERATION.

Ashleigh
Brilliant

POT-SHOTS NO. 278

DUE TO CIRCUMSTANCES
BEYOND MY CONTROL,
I AM MASTER OF MY FATE
AND CAPTAIN OF MY SOUL.

Ashleigh Brilliant.com

POT-SHOTS NO. 118

I'M JUST
MOVING CLOUDS
TODAY —

TOMORROW
I'LL TRY
MOUNTAINS.

Ashleigh
Brilliant
.COM

POT-SHOTS NO. 16

HOW MUCH MORE OF
THE PRESENT DO WE
HAVE TO SIT THROUGH
BEFORE THE FUTURE
COMES ON?

Ashleigh
Brilliant
.COM

©ASHLEIGH BRILLIANT 1981.

POT-SHOTS NO. 2267.

Ashleigh
Brilliant
.com

HAVING LIVED THROUGH SOME BAD TIMES,

I'M LIVING PROOF THAT SOME BAD TIMES CAN BE LIVED THROUGH.

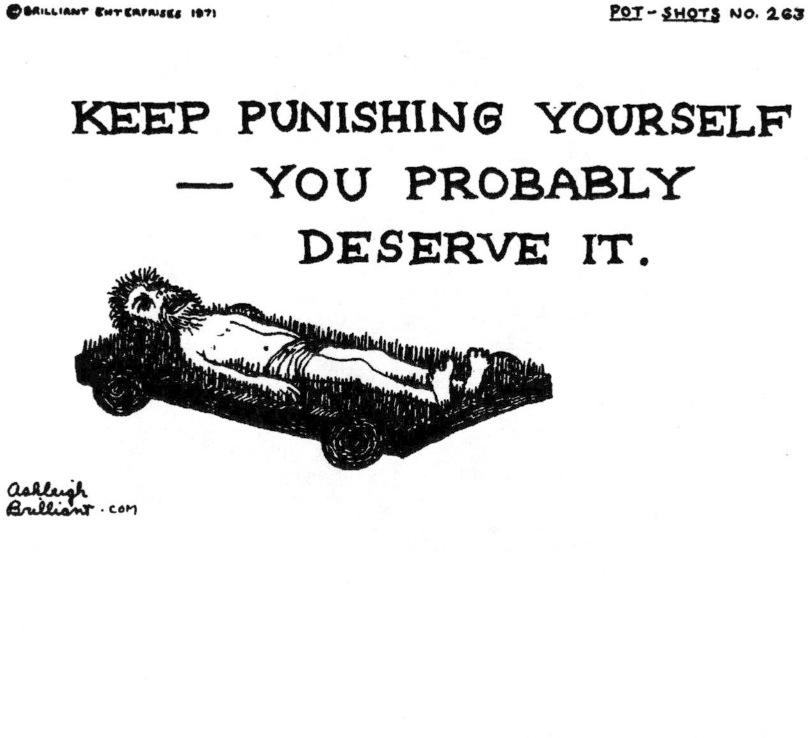

©BRILLIANT ENTERPRISES 1971

POT-SHOTS NO. 263

KEEP PUNISHING YOURSELF — YOU PROBABLY DESERVE IT.

Ashleigh
Brilliant . com

POT-SHOTS NO. 283

I'M IN SEARCH
OF MYSELF —

HAVE YOU SEEN ME ANYWHERE?

  POT-SHOTS NO. 310

I BLAME
MYSELF
FOR NOT
BLAMING YOU SOONER

ASHLEIGH BRILLIANT 1981.

POT-SHOTS NO. 2258.

ALL I NEED TODAY

IS ENOUGH TO GET ME AS FAR AS TOMORROW.

©ASHLEIGH BRILLIANT 1981.

POT-SHOTS NO. 2259.

ONCE I WANTED TOTAL HAPPINESS ~

NOW I WILL SETTLE FOR A LITTLE LESS PAIN.

Ashleigh Brilliant.com

© ASHLEIGH BRILLIANT 1981.

POT-SHOTS NO. 2247.

TOMORROW IS ANOTHER DAY ~

BUT I HOPE IT'S NOT ANOTHER DAY LIKE THIS ONE.

Ashleigh Brilliant

© ASHLEIGH BRILLIANT 1981.

POT-SHOTS NO. 2237.

TO BE PERFECTLY HONEST,

I SOMETIMES FIND IT VERY DIFFICULT TO BE PERFECTLY HONEST.

Ashleigh Brilliant · com

© ASHLEIGH BRILLIANT 1981.

IT'S ALWAYS GOOD TO SEE A FRIENDLY FACE ~

COULD YOU MAKE YOURS A LITTLE FRIENDLIER?

Ashleigh Brilliant™.com

POT-SHOTS NO. 2205.

HOW MUCH OF THE INTOLERABLE SHOULD I TOLERATE,

SIMPLY IN ORDER TO BE POLITE?

Ashleigh Brilliant .com

© ASHLEIGH BRILLIANT 1981.

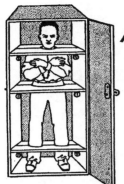

©ASHLEIGH BRILLIANT 1981.

POT-SHOTS NO. 2120.

SLAVERY AND TORTURE WERE OUTLAWED LONG AGO,

BUT, FOR SOME REASON, MARRIAGE IS STILL LEGAL.

Ashleigh Brilliant · com

Ashleigh Brilliant · com

POT-SHOTS NO. 508

TRY TO RELAX AND ENJOY THE CRISIS.

©BRILLIANT ENTERPRISES 1974

©BRILLIANT ENTERPRISES 1974

POT-SHOTS NO. 533

How kind of you to want to live my life for me.

Ashleigh Brilliant .com

© ASHLEIGH BRILLIANT 1981.

POT-SHOTS NO. 2115.

I SOMETIMES GIVE VERY CAREFUL CONSIDERATION TO THE RIGHT,

BEFORE DOING THE WRONG.

Ashleigh Brilliant .com

ASHLEIGH BRILLIANT 1981.

POT-SHOTS NO. 2113

WE'RE IN THIS TOGETHER,

BUT THERE'S ALWAYS ROOM FOR ONE LESS.

Ashleig Brill...

© ASHLEIGH BRILLIANT 1981.   POT-SHOTS NO. 2084.

OF COURSE I KNOW WHAT REALITY IS~

I JUST CAN'T PUT IT INTO THOUGHTS.

Ashleigh Brilliant .COM

POT-SHOTS NO. 2099.

IT FRIGHTENS ME

Ashleigh Brilliant .com

WHEN YOU, VERY SUDDENLY, START TO BEHAVE SENSIBLY.

© BRILLIANT ENTERPRISES 1976. POT-SHOTS NO. 898.

Time
will end
all my
troubles,

but I don't
always
approve of
Time's
methods.

Ashleigh
Brilliant

© ASHLEIGH BRILLIANT 1980. POT-SHOTS NO. 1902.

ONE OF MY CLEVER WAYS
OF FIGHTING BACK
AGAINST
THE
WORLD

IS BY
BOLDLY
GOING TO BED.

Ashleigh Brilliant.com

©ASHLEIGH BRILLIANT 1981.

POT-SHOTS NO. 2307.

I FEEL TIRED,
after my long journey through the past ten years.

Ashleigh
Brilliant
.com

POT-SHOTS NO. 2314.

WHAT IS THIS "REAL LIFE" I KEEP HEARING ABOUT?

©ASHLEIGH BRILLIANT 1981.

Ashleigh Brilliant.com

© BRILLIANT ENTERPRISES 1977

POT-SHOTS NO. 1064.

What is it like to be You?

Ashleigh
Brilliant
.com

POT-SHOTS NO. 2070.

Ashleigh
Brilliant
.com

MOST OF WHAT I KNOW ABOUT HAPPINESS AND MISERY

I'VE LEARNED SINCE I MET YOU.

© ASHLEIGH BRILLIANT 1981.

POT-SHOTS NO. 2322.

WOULD YOU CARE TO VIEW THE RUINS OF MY GOOD INTENTIONS?

© ASHLEIGH BRILLIANT 1981.

Ashleigh Brilliant.com

© ASHLEIGH BRILLIANT 1981.

POT-SHOTS NO. 2336.

LIFE

IS NOT NECESSARILY
SOMETHING I WOULD
RECOMMEND
TO EVERYBODY.

Ashleigh Brilliant.com

© ASHLEIGH BRILLIANT 1981.

POT-SHOTS NO. 2345.

MY STRATEGY

IS, WHENEVER POSSIBLE,
TO
KEEP OUT OF
THE ARENA.

Ashleigh Brilliant.com

© ASHLEIGH BRILLIANT 1981.

POT-SHOTS NO. 2212.

DON'T LET YOURSELF SUFFER NEEDLESSLY ~

FIND
A NEED
TO SUFFER.

Ashleigh Brilliant
.com

POT-SHOTS NO. 2346.

IF MY LIFE
HAD BEEN
EASIER TO LIVE,

I MIGHT ALREADY
HAVE FINISHED
LIVING IT.

© ASHLEIGH BRILLIANT 1981.

Ashleigh
Brilliant.com

© ASHLEIGH BRILLIANT 1982.

POT-SHOTS NO. 2406.

MY
GREAT
AMBITION
IS
TO SECURE
A
SPEAKING PART
IN
MY OWN LIFE.

Ashleigh Brilliant
.com

POT-SHOTS NO. 2413.

YESTERDAY,
    UPON MY BACK,
YOUR BURDEN
SUDDENLY
    APPEARED ~

HOW DID
YOU DO IT?

©ASHLEIGH BRILLIANT 1982

POT-SHOTS NO. 2379.

IN ORDER
    FOR ME
TO DO BETTER
NEXT TIME,
ONE THING
IS ESSENTIAL:

TO
SURVIVE
THIS
TIME.

POT-SHOTS NO. 2630.

WHY
DO I
KEEP
COMING
HOME,
EVERY TIME
I TRY
TO TRACE
MY TROUBLES
TO THEIR
SOURCE?

©ASHLEIGH BRILLIANT 1982.

POT-SHOTS NO. 2493.

SOMETIMES
I WISH
I COULD GIVE
ALL MY
EMOTIONS

THE DAY
OFF.

NO. 2668.

NEXT
TIME,

I INTEND
TO BE
THOROUGHLY
PREPARED

FOR LAST TIME.

© ASHLEIGH BRILLIANT 1982.

POT-SHOTS NO. 2446

If you tire of your dreams,

REALITY IS ALWAYS AVAILABLE AT NO EXTRA CHARGE.

Ashleigh Brilliant.com

© ASHLEIGH BRILLIANT 1982.

POT-SHOTS NO. 2571.
Ashleigh Brilliant .com

I'LL FACE THE PROBLEM OF HOW TO LIVE

WHEN I COME TO IT.

POT-SHOTS NO. 2867   ©ASHLEIGH BRILLIANT 1983.

DON'T
EXPECT ME
TO STRAIGHTEN UP,
WHEN
IT'S ALL I CAN DO
TO KEEP FROM
FALLING OVER.

Ashleigh
Brilliant.com

POT-SHOTS NO. 2992.

I WOULD
LIKE TO SPEAK
TO WHOEVER
IS IN CONTROL
OF MY LIFE,

AND SUGGEST
SOME
IMPROVEMENTS.

Ashleigh
Brilliant.com

©ASHLEIGH BRILLIANT 1983.

POT-SHOTS NO. 2798.

SOMETHING
IN ME
STILL FEELS
THE SAME WAY
I DID
BEFORE I
CHANGED MY MIND.

© ASHLEIGH BRILLIANT 1983

© ASHLEIGH BRILLIANT 1983.

POT-SHOTS NO. 2770.

BY WHAT
PROCESS
DID I
BECOME
A STRANGER
IN
MY OWN
LIFE?

Ashleigh
Brilliant.

© ASHLEIGH BRILLIANT 1983.

POT-SHOTS NO. 2857.

WHY IS IT SO MUCH EASIER
TO PREDICT
THE MOVEMENTS
OF PLANETS
THAN
THE
BEHAVIOR
OF PEOPLE?

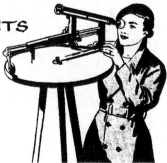

© ASHLEIGH BRILLIANT 1983.

POT-SHOTS NO. 2887.
Ashleigh Brilliant.com

IN SOME CASES,
A BROKEN HEART
PROVES
TO BE
ONLY A
SUPERFICIAL
WOUND.

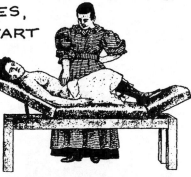

© ASHLEIGH BRILLIANT 1983.

POT-SHOTS NO. 2960.

SOMETIMES
MY MIND
IS SO
UNCOMFORTABLE,

I WISH
I COULD
GO SOMEWHERE
AND
TAKE IT OFF.

Ashleigh Brilliant.com

© ASHLEIGH BRILLIANT 1983.

POT-SHOTS NO. 2973.

YOU CAN FEEL
GREAT MUSIC
WITHOUT
HEARING IT,

AND
YOU CAN FEEL
GREAT TRUTH
WITHOUT
UNDERSTANDING IT.

Ashleigh Brilliant.com

©ASHLEIGH BRILLIANT 1983.

POT-SHOTS NO. 2976.
Ashleigh
Brilliant
.com

ALLOW ME
TO CONGRATULATE YOU
ON THE SKILL
WITH WHICH
YOU HIDE
YOUR
DEFECTS.

©ASHLEIGH BRILLIANT 1983.

POT-SHOTS NO. 3106.

I'VE BEEN TRYING
DESPERATELY
TO SAVE
MY MARRIAGE
FOR
THE LAST
35 YEARS.

Ashleigh
Brilliant.com

©ASHLEIGH BRILLIANT 1983.

POT-SHOTS NO. 3122.

IT'S NOT THAT
I DON'T TRUST YOU

— OR
IS IT?

© ASHLEIGH BRILLIANT 1985.

POT-SHOTS NO. 3190.

BY THE TIME YOU REALIZE WHAT LOVE CAN DO,

THE DAMAGE HAS USUALLY ALREADY BEEN DONE.

Ashleigh Brilliant .com

© ASHLEIGH BRILLIANT 1985.

POT-SHOTS NO. 3204.

Ashleigh Brilliant .com

HOW MUCH MUST I CHANGE TO SATISFY YOU? ~

AND WOULD ANYTHING BE LEFT OF THE ORIGINAL ME?

POT-SHOTS NO. 3205.

WHAT I MOST NEED AT THIS POINT IN MY LIFE

IS TO HAVE HAD A BETTER CHILDHOOD.

Ashleigh Brilliant .com

© ASHLEIGH BRILLIANT 1985.

© ASHLEIGH BRILLIANT 1985.   AshleighBrilliant.com   POT-SHOTS NO. 3207.

MY LIFE IS VERY DELICATELY BALANCED:

PLEASE DON'T MAKE ANY SUDDEN MOVEMENTS.

© ASHLEIGH BRILLIANT 1985.   POT-SHOTS NO. 3284.

HOW CAN I WAKE YOU UP,

WITHOUT SHATTERING YOUR DREAMS?

© ASHLEIGH BRILLIANT 1985.

POT-SHOTS NO. 3308.

IF KNOWLEDGE IS POWER,

WHY DO SO MANY OF THE THINGS I KNOW MAKE ME FEEL POWERLESS?

AshleighBrilliant.com

POT-SHOTS NO. 3299.

Ashleigh Brilliant .com

MANY PAST WRONGS

CAN NEVER BE RIGHTED,

~ BUT MANY FUTURE WRONGS CAN STILL BE PREVENTED.

© ASHLEIGH BRILLIANT 1985.

© ASHLEIGH BRILLIANT 1985.   POT-SHOTS NO. 3210.

THE EXACT LOCATION OF HELL IS NOT WELL-KNOWN,

EXCEPT
TO THOSE
OF US
WHO'VE
BEEN THERE.

Ashleigh Brilliant .com

POT-SHOTS NO. 3222

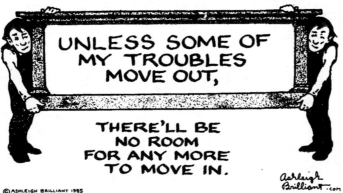

UNLESS SOME OF MY TROUBLES MOVE OUT,

THERE'LL BE
NO ROOM
FOR ANY MORE
TO MOVE IN.

Ashleigh Brilliant .com

© ASHLEIGH BRILLIANT 1985

POT-SHOTS NO. 3237.

MY LIFE
SO FAR
HAS BEEN
A LONG
SERIES
OF
THINGS
I WASN'T
READY FOR.

Ashleigh Brilliant .com

© ASHLEIGH BRILLIANT 1985.

POT-SHOTS NO. 3302.

SOMETIMES
I WONDER

IF
THE WORLD
REALLY
HAS
MY BEST
INTERESTS
AT HEART.

© ASHLEIGH BRILLIANT 1985.

POT-SHOTS NO. 3323

IN SOME
UNFORTUNATE
CASES,

THE ONLY WAY
TO EXPRESS LOVE

IS SIMPLY
TO LEAVE
THE PERSON
ALONE.

POT-SHOTS NO. 3327

IT'S HARD
TO DECIDE
WHAT TO DO,

BUT I SOLVE IT
BY NOT
DOING ANYTHING.

© ASHLEIGH BRILLIANT 1985

YOU
HAVE
YOUR
PROBLEMS,

AND I
HAVE
YOURS.

POT-
SHOTS
NO. 3376

Ashleigh
Brilliant

THE LESS
ANYBODY
WANTS YOU,

THE LESS
VALUABLE
YOU BECOME,

UNLESS
YOU REALLY
WANT
YOURSELF.

©ASHLEIGH BRILLIANT 1985.

POT-SHOTS NO. 3438.

THE THINGS I'M PRAYING FOR

SOMETIMES MATTER LESS THAN THE THINGS I'M PRAYING AGAINST.

POT-SHOTS NO. 3466.

I DIDN'T KNOW PEOPLE LIKE YOU WERE STILL BEING PRODUCED.

©ASHLEIGH BRILLIANT 1985.

POT-SHOTS NO. 3352

Where
I come from
and where
I belong
are
not necessarily
the same
place.

Ashleigh
Brilliant
.com

POT-SHOTS NO. 3387.

I KNEW
SOMETHING
WAS WRONG
THE MOMENT
YOU BIT
MY NOSE.

Ashleigh Brilliant
.com

POT-SHOTS NO. 3392.

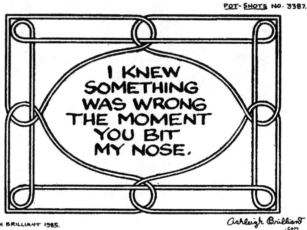

IF YOU HAVE
THE SAME KIND
OF PROBLEMS
I HAVE,

PLEASE SEEK HELP
IMMEDIATELY!

Ashleigh
Brilliant.com

©ASHLEIGH BRILLIANT 1985. POT-SHOTS NO. 3437.

IT'S GOOD
TO KNOW
I CAN ALWAYS
DEPEND ON
YOUR
HALF-HEARTED
SUPPORT.

Ashleigh
Brilliant
.com

ASHLEIGH BRILLIANT 1985. POT-SHOTS NO. 3470.

I WANT
TO
TAKE HOLD
OF
REALITY~
BUT
SOMEBODY
KEEPS
MOVING IT.

Ashleigh
Brilliant
.com

© ASHLEIGH
BRILLIANT 1985 POT-SHOTS NO. 3440.

ONE PROBLEM
I HAVE
DEFINITELY
SOLVED
IS
THE PROBLEM
OF NOT HAVING
ENOUGH
TO WORRY ABOUT.

Ashleigh
Brilliant
.com

POT-SHOTS NO. 3475.

JUST BECAUSE I LOVE YOU

DOESN'T NECESSARILY MEAN I FIND IT EASY TO TOLERATE YOU.

POT-SHOTS NO. 3500.

Ashleigh Brilliant.com

MY DREAMS ARE NOT DEAD ~

THEY'RE ONLY SLEEPING.

© ASHLEIGH BRILLIANT 1987.   POT-SHOTS NO. 4027.

IT'S
SURPRISING
HOW FAR
YOU CAN GO
THROUGH LIFE

WITHOUT
EVER HAVING
WHAT YOU
REALLY
NEED.

© ASHLEIGH BRILLIANT 1988.   Ashleigh Brilliant.com   POT-SHOTS NO. 4337.

WHAT'S
CONFUSING
ABOUT
MY
LIFE STORY

IS THAT
THE PLOT
BEGAN
BEFORE
I CAME
ON
THE SCENE.

© ASHLEIGH BRILLIANT 1985.

POT-SHOTS NO. 5466.

MY ROAD'S BEEN MOSTLY UPHILL,

BUT
AT LEAST
THAT MAKES
IT EASIER
IF I WANT
TO STOP.

Ashleigh Brilliant .com

© ASHLEIGH BRILLIANT 1987.

POT-SHOTS NO. 4126.

I UNDERSTOOD MOST OF YOUR MESSAGE,

BUT
WOULD YOU MIND
REPEATING
THE LAST SCREAM?

Ashleigh Brilliant .com

©ASHLEIGH BRILLIANT 1988.　　　　　　　　POT-SHOTS NO.4367.

I wish
relationships
could be
tested
in advance
for safety,
comfort,
and
durability.

©ASHLEIGH BRILLIANT 1988.　　　　　　POT-SHOTS NO.4374.

ANYTHING CAN HAPPEN
TO ME TOMORROW,

BUT
AT LEAST
NOTHING MORE
CAN HAPPEN
TO ME
YESTERDAY.

POT-SHOTS NO.4378.

WHAT
YOU OWE
TO
YOURSELF

CAN BE
VERY DIFFICULT
TO COLLECT.

©ASHLEIGH BRILLIANT 1988.

©ASHLEIGH BRILLIANT 1988.

POT-SHOTS NO.4416

PEOPLE WHO NEED TO RECEIVE CARE

ARE USEFUL AND NECESSARY TO PEOPLE WHO NEED TO GIVE IT.

©ASHLEIGH BRILLIANT 1988.

POT-SHOTS NO.4437.

YOU'D BE SURPRISED TO KNOW HOW MANY DIFFERENT WAYS THERE ARE TO BE HURT BY YOU.

Ashleigh Brilliant.com

POT-SHOTS NO. 4575.

THE ONLY WAY OUT OF SOME TROUBLES

IS NEVER TO GET INTO THEM.

© ASHLEIGH BRILLIANT 1988.   Ashleigh Brilliant .com

© ASHLEIGH BRILLIANT 1988.   Ashleigh Brilliant .com   POT-SHOTS NO. 4508.

IF MY LIFE CAN'T HAVE BOTH COMFORT AND MEANING,

I'D PREFER MEANINGLESS COMFORT TO UNCOMFORTABLE MEANING.

POT-SHOTS NO. 4387.   Ashleigh Brilliant.com

WHAT I NEED
IS
A MAP
OF
YOUR MIND,

WITH
DANGEROUS
AREAS
CLEARLY
MARKED.

©ASHLEIGH BRILLIANT 1988.

©ASHLEIGH BRILLIANT 1988.

POT-SHOTS NO. 4445.

SOMETIMES
THE ONLY WAY
TO DEAL WITH
MY PROBLEMS

IS
TO
TAKE
THEM
NONE
AT A
TIME.

Ashleigh Brilliant.com

POT-SHOTS NO. 4489.

I LOVE
MY
FAMILY,

AND
WOULD DO
ANYTHING
TO KEEP THEM
FROM HURTING ME.

©ASHLEIGH BRILLIANT 1988

© ASHLEIGH BRILLIANT 1988. POT-SHOTS NO. 4538.

WHAT BINDS US MOST STRONGLY TOGETHER

IS
OUR LONG HISTORY
OF CONFLICT
WITH EACH OTHER.

Ashleigh
Brilliant.com

© ASHLEIGH BRILLIANT 1988. POT-SHOTS NO. 4545.

MY FIRST LINE OF DEFENSE AGAINST REALITY

IS
CALLED
SLEEP.

Ashleigh Brilliant
.com

© ASHLEIGH BRILLIANT 1988. POT-SHOTS NO. 4551.

Despite all modern safeguards,

many marriages
continue to be
the result
of
human error.

Ashleigh Brilliant .com

© ASHLEIGH BRILLIANT 1988.   POT-SHOTS NO. 4690.

VIOLENT PEOPLE ARE RELATIVELY EASY TO HANDLE~

IT'S CALM REASONABLE PEOPLE WHO ARE THE GREAT HIDDEN DANGER.

© ASHLEIGH BRILLIANT 1988.   POT-SHOTS NO. 4712.

WHENEVER I'M ALONE WITH YOU,

WHY DO I ALWAYS FEEL OUTNUMBERED?

ISN'T THERE
SOME WAY
TO GET
THE WISDOM
OF HINDSIGHT
IN ADVANCE?

Ashleigh Brilliant.com

SOMETIMES
IT'S HARD
TO REMEMBER
WHY
I LOVE YOU,

CAN YOU
GIVE ME
A HINT?

Ashleigh Brilliant.com

UNTIL
I MET YOU,

I THOUGHT
THE WORLD HAD
SOME RATIONAL BASIS.

Ashleigh Brilliant.com

© ASHLEIGH BRILLIANT 1989. POT-SHOTS NO. 4924.

NEVER TRY
TO PUT YOURSELF
IN THE
OTHER PERSON'S
POSITION ~

IT
WILL
ONLY
CONFUSE YOU.

Ashleigh Brilliant.com
SANTA BARBARA

© ASHLEIGH BRILLIANT 1989. POT-SHOTS NO. 4811.

NOBODY EVER

COMES
OUT OF

A SUCCESSFUL MARRIAGE
VOLUNTARILY.

Ashleigh
Brilliant.com
SANTA BARBARA

© ASHLEIGH BRILLIANT 1989. POT-SHOTS NO. 4882.

NO! NO!
FOR GOD'S SAKE,
DON'T USE
YOUR OWN
BEST JUDGMENT!

Ashleigh Brilliant.com
SANTA BARBARA

POT-SHOTS NO. 4774.

AT WHAT STAGE OF MY LIFE CYCLE AM I SUPPOSED TO FIND HAPPINESS?

© ASHLEIGH BRILLIANT 1988.

Ashleigh Brilliant .com

© ASHLEIGH BRILLIANT 1988.

POT-SHOTS NO. 4779.

Ashleigh Brilliant .com

FOR PERMANENT HAPPINESS

FIND A MOMENT IN WHICH ALL IS WELL, AND REFUSE TO LEAVE IT.

POT-SHOTS NO. 4855. ©ASHLEIGH BRILLIANT 1989.

SOME PEOPLE SHOULD BE REQUIRED TO WEAR WARNING-SIGNS.

DANGER

Ashleigh Brilliant.com
SANTA BARBARA

©ASHLEIGH BRILLIANT 1989.

POT-SHOTS NO. 4858.

Ashleigh Brilliant.com
SANTA BARBARA

HOW MUCH MORE MUST I INVEST IN THIS RELATIONSHIP,

BEFORE I GET BACK ANYTHING WORTH HAVING?

© ASHLEIGH BRILLIANT 1989. POT-SHOTS NO. 4971.

THERE IS A SADNESS IN MY HEAD,

WHICH COULD BE FATAL IF IT SPREADS TO MY HEART.

Ashleigh Brilliant.com
SANTA BARBARA

© ASHLEIGH BRILLIANT 1990. POT-SHOTS NO. 5041.

IT WOULD SAVE A LOT OF EFFORT,

IF I COULD OPERATE MYSELF BY REMOTE CONTROL.

Ashleigh Brilliant.com
SANTA BARBARA

© ASHLEIGH BRILLIANT 1990. POT-SHOTS NO. 5106.

Ashleigh Brilliant.com
SANTA BARBARA

WHY DO I UNDERSTAND YOU SO MUCH BETTER

WHEN I LOSE ALL CONTACT WITH REALITY?

©ASHLEIGH BRILLIANT 1991.   POT-SHOTS NO. 5382.

OH HOW I REGRET
THAT I CAN'T
DEVOTE
MY ENTIRE LIFE
TO
YOU AND
YOUR PROBLEMS.

Ashleigh Brilliant.com
SANTA BARBARA

©ASHLEIGH BRILLIANT 1991.   POT-SHOTS NO. 5330.

WHICH IS
MORE SAD:

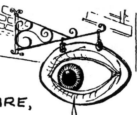

TO LOSE
YOUR HEART'S DESIRE,

OR TO FIND IT
NO LONGER DESIRABLE?

Ashleigh
Brilliant.com
SANTA BARBARA

©ASHLEIGH BRILLIANT 1991.   POT-SHOTS NO. 5517.

CONGRATULATE
ME!

I've just had
another
narrow
escape
from reality.

Ashleigh Brilliant.com
SANTA BARBARA

©ASHLEIGH BRILLIANT 1989. POT-SHOTS NO. 4977.

FORGIVE ME

FOR FINDING IT IMPOSSIBLE TO FORGIVE YOU.

Ashleigh Brilliant.com
SANTA BARBARA

©ASHLEIGH BRILLIANT 1989. POT-SHOTS NO. 4984.

WE ARE UNITED IN OUR DETERMINATION

Ashleigh Brilliant.com
SANTA BARBARA

TO GO OUR SEPARATE WAYS.

© ASHLEIGH BRILLIANT 1990.

POT-SHOTS NO. 5248.

MUST I RISK MY OWN SANITY in trying to rescue yours?

© ASHLEIGH BRILLIANT 1991.

POT-SHOTS NO. 5447.

WHY DOES OUR BEING TOGETHER ALWAYS SEEM TO REQUIRE THE PRESENCE OF A REFEREE?

POT-SHOTS NO. 5927.

SOMETIMES IT REQUIRES A VERY CLEAR DAY
IN ORDER TO SEE THE OBVIOUS.

Ashleigh Brilliant.com
SANTA BARBARA

POT-SHOTS NO. 5995.

I WASN'T REALLY ME

UNTIL I GOT AWAY FROM YOU.

Ashleigh Brilliant .com

POT-SHOTS NO. 5961.

DON'T FACE REALITY~

IT'S TERRIBLY DISAPPOINTING.

Ashleigh Brilliant .com

© ASHLEIGH BRILLIANT 1990.

POT-SHOTS NO. 5221.

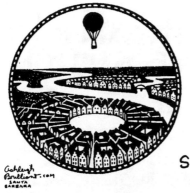

TO
FIND OUT
WHERE
YOU ARE,

IT IS
SOMETIMES
NECESSARY
TO GO
SOMEWHERE ELSE.

© ASHLEIGH BRILLIANT 1993. SANTA BARBARA.

POT-SHOTS NO. 6227.

NO MATTER
HOW MANY
GOOD STEPS
YOU TAKE,

A SINGLE
BAD ONE
CAN END
YOUR WHOLE
JOURNEY.

© ASHLEIGH BRILLIANT 1990.

POT-SHOTS NO. 5023.

IT'S HARD TO KNOW
EXACTLY WHICH WAY
TO TURN

IN ORDER
TO FACE
REALITY.

AshleighBrilliant.com

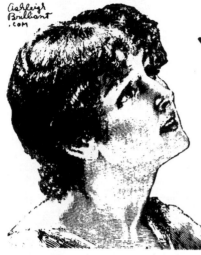

©ASHLEIGH BRILLIANT 1992 SANTA BARBARA

Ashleigh Brilliant .com

POT-SHOTS NO. 5639.

I WANT VERY MUCH TO UNDERSTAND YOU,

BECAUSE FOR ME THAT WOULD BE A TOTALLY NEW EXPERIENCE.

POT-SHOTS NO. 5877. ©ASHLEIGH BRILLIANT 1992.

MY BIGGEST REGRET ABOUT THE THINGS I'VE DONE

IS THAT I DIDN'T DO SOME OF THEM SOONER.

Ashleigh Brilliant.com CANTA BARBARA

©ASHLEIGH BRILLIANT 1993. SANTA BARBARA.

POT-SHOTS NO. 6309.

THE BEST
WAY
I CAN HELP
CERTAIN
PEOPLE

IS BY
LETTING THEM
FEEL
SUPERIOR
TO ME.

©ASHLEIGH BRILLIANT 1993. SANTA BARBARA.

POT-SHOTS NO. 6238.

Ashleigh Brilliant .com

IF YOU MUST
WASTE
YOUR LIFE,

TRY
TO DO IT
IN A CREATIVE
AND
ORIGINAL WAY.

©ASHLEIGH BRILLIANT 1996. SANTA BARBARA.

POT-SHOTS NO. 7421.

I WOULDN'T LOVE YOU
SO MUCH,

Ashleigh Brilliant .com

IF
THERE WERE
ANYTHING
I COULD
DO
ABOUT IT.

©ASHLEIGH BRILLIANT 1995. SANTA BARBARA.

POT-SHOTS NO. 6776.

WHY DO I SUFFER
THE SAME
PAINFUL
CONSEQUENCES,

EVERY TIME
I PERFORM
THE SAME
FOOLISH
ACTS?

©ASHLEIGH BRILLIANT 1995.

POT-SHOTS
NO. 6907.

MY
BIGGEST
PROBLEM

IS THAT
I HAVE
NO ONE TO BLAME
BUT MYSELF.

Ashleigh Brilliant.com
SANTA BARBARA

©ASHLEIGH BRILLIANT 1995. SANTA BARBARA.

POT-SHOTS NO. 6737.

YES, BUT IT'S ONLY MY
UNREALISTIC
EXPECTATIONS

THAT ARE
KEEPING ME
ALIVE.

Ashleigh
Brilliant
.com

POT-SHOTS NO. 6197.

THINGS ARE SOMETIMES BETTER LEFT AS THEY ARE,

Ashleigh
Brilliant .com

BUT
YOU CAN'T
BE SURE
UNTIL YOU
CHANGE
THEM.

POT-SHOTS NO. 6893.

SOME
PEOPLE
GET THEIR
GREATEST
SATISFACTION
FROM
HELPING
OTHERS ~

OTHERS
GET
THEIRS
FROM
BEING
HELPED.

Ashleigh Brilliant .com
SANTA BARBARA

© ASHLEIGH BRILLIANT 1995. Ashleigh Brilliant SANTA BARBARA. POT-SHOTS NO. 6606.

HOW WRONG MUST THINGS GET,
BEFORE THEY'RE WORTH ALL THE TROUBLE OF TRYING TO SET RIGHT?

© ASHLEIGH BRILLIANT 1996.
SANTA BARBARA

POT-SHOTS NO. 7062.

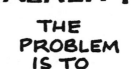

MY BEAUTIFUL FANTASIES FLOAT ON A SEA OF REALITY~
THE PROBLEM IS TO PREVENT LEAKS.

Ashleigh Brilliant .com

© ASHLEIGH BRILLIANT 1996. SANTA BARBARA.

POT-SHOTS NO. 7088.

WHY AM I SO EASILY DECEIVED

BY PEOPLE WHO TELL ME WHAT I DESPERATELY WANT TO BELIEVE?

Ashleigh Brilliant.com

© ASHLEIGH BRILLIANT 1996. SANTA BARBARA.

POT-SHOTS NO. 7108.

IT'S HARD PLAYING MY PART IN LIFE,

BECAUSE MANY OTHER PLAYERS ARE APPARENTLY USING A DIFFERENT SCRIPT.

© ASHLEIGH BRILLIANT 1996. SANTA BARBARA

POT-SHOTS NO. 7504.

I KNOW WHAT REALITY IS~

I'VE BEEN THERE — I DIDN'T LIKE IT.

© ASHLEIGH BRILLIANT 1998.
SANTA BARBARA

POT-SHOTS NO. 7589.

I COULD NEVER HAVE COME SO FAR

WITHOUT YOUR CONSTANT RESISTANCE.

Ashleigh Brilliant
.com

© ASHLEIGH BRILLIANT 1998.
SANTA BARBARA

POT-SHOTS NO. 7789.

LIFE MAY BE TRYING TO TELL ME SOMETHING,

BUT I'M AFRAID IT'S NOT A FRIENDLY MESSAGE.

Ashleigh Brilliant .com

© ASHLEIGH BRILLIANT 1998.

POT-SHOTS NO. 7627.

DON'T LEAVE ME!

OR I MAY REALIZE HOW LITTLE I EVER NEEDED YOU.

Ashleigh Brilliant .com
SANTA BARBARA

© ASHLEIGH BRILLIANT 1996 SANTA BARBARA

POT-SHOTS NO. 7089.

IT ONLY HURTS

WHEN I THINK OR FEEL.

© ASHLEIGH BRILLIANT 1993 · SANTA BARBARA.

POT-SHOTS NO. 6354.

MY HEAD NEVER LIES TO MY HEART ~

Ashleigh Brilliant .com

BUT MY HEART SOMETIMES TELLS LITTLE FIBS TO MY HEAD.

©ASHLEIGH BRILLIANT 1998.

POT-SHOTS NO. 7599.

IF YOU MUST MARRY,

TRY TO MARRY SOMEONE YOU CAN LIVE WITH.

AshleighBrilliant.com
SANTA BARBARA

AshleighBrilliant.com
SANTA BARBARA

©ASHLEIGH BRILLIANT 1996.

POT-SHOTS NO. 7285.

YOUR VIRTUES BLIND ME TO YOUR FAULTS,

BUT ALAS, ONLY IN ONE EYE.

POT-SHOTS NO. 7662.

I SINCERELY
WANT TO
BELIEVE
IN REALITY,

BUT OTHER THINGS
KEEP GETTING IN THE WAY.

AshleighBrilliant.com

POT-SHOTS NO. 7707.

Ashleigh
Brilliant.com
SANTA
BARBARA

HOW CAN
LIFE BE
SO SAD

AND SO
RIDICULOUS

AT THE
SAME TIME?

POT-SHOTS NO. 7724.

I'VE LOOKED
ALL OVER ~

WHERE CAN I
FIND SOME
INNER
STRENGTH?

AshleighBrilliant.com

POT-SHOTS NO. 7781.

SOUNDS OF ANGUISH AND HOSTILITY!

— I MUST BE GETTING NEAR HOME.

Ashleigh Brilliant.com

POT-SHOTS NO. 7768.

Ashleigh Brilliant .com

THE FACTS MAY BE AGAINST ME,

but all the illusions are on my side.

POT-SHOTS NO. 7862.

WHY AM I SO OFTEN UNCERTAIN

WHAT TO HOLD ON TO

AND WHAT TO LET GO OF?

Ashleigh Brilliant.com
SANTA BARBARA

POT-SHOTS NO. 7870.

SELF-PRESERVATION IS THE FIRST LAW OF NATURE,

BUT IT'S NOT ALWAYS CONSIDERED GOOD MANNERS.

Ashleigh Brilliant.com

POT-SHOTS NO. 8016.

IF I DIDN'T KEEP MY EMOTIONS UNDER CONTROL,

THEY WOULD ALWAYS BE DRAGGING ME TOWARDS YOU.

POT-SHOTS NO. 8090.

THANK YOU FOR RUINING MY LIFE~

IT WAS A GREAT EXPERIENCE.

Ashleigh Brilliant .com

POT-SHOTS NO. 8065.

SOME OF THE PROMISES I'VE MADE TO MYSELF

WERE MADE UNDER DURESS.

Ashleigh Brilliant .com

POT-SHOTS NO. 7927.

THERE WAS A TIME WHEN MY TROUBLES WERE INCOMPLETE~

THEN YOU CAME ALONG.

ashleigh Brilliant.com

POT-SHOTS NO. 8010.

THE PROBLEMS OCCUPY SO MUCH SPACE IN MY LIFE

THAT THERE'S NO ROOM FOR THE SOLUTIONS.

ashleigh Brilliant.com SANTA BARBARA.

© ASHLEIGH BRILLIANT 1998. SANTA BARBARA.

POT-SHOTS NO. 7544.

THERE'S NO SUCH THING AS THE RIGHT TO BE COMFORTABLE — BUT THERE OUGHT TO BE!

Ashleigh Brilliant.com

© ASHLEIGH BRILLIANT 1985.

POT-SHOTS NO. 3484.

WHERE SHOULD I STAND TO GET THE BEST VIEW OF REALITY?

Ashleigh Brilliant .com

© BRILLIANT ENTERPRISES 1971

POT-SHOTS No. 294

I AM HOPING
VERY SOON
TO HAVE
SOMETHING
TO HOPE FOR.

Ashleigh Brilliant.com

© ASHLEIGH BRILLIANT 1980.

POT-SHOTS NO. 1761.

COULD IT
POSSIBLY BE
THAT
YOUR PURPOSE
IN LIFE
IS
TO GIVE ME
TROUBLE?

Ashleigh
Brilliant
.com

THE
BPD SPEAKS

POT-SHOTS NO. 159 ©BRILLIANT ENTERPRISES 1970

Ashleigh
Brilliant.com

©ASHLEIGH BRILLIANT 1980.

POT-SHOTS NO. 1696.

ONE GOOD REASON
FOR TRUSTING ME
IS THAT
MANY OTHER
FOOLISH PEOPLE
ALREADY
TRUST ME.

Ashleigh
Brilliant.com

© BRILLIANT ENTERPRISES 1971

POT-SHOTS NO. 226.

REJOICE!

I AM COMING!

Ashleigh
Brilliant.com

POT-SHOTS NO. 1936.

In order
to appear
completely
spontaneous,
my act
requires
very careful
rehearsal.

© ASHLEIGH BRILLIANT 1980.

© BRILLIANT ENTERPRISES 1969.

POT-SHOTS NO. 57

Ashleigh
Brilliant
.com

BEEN THROUGH HELL?

AND WHAT DID YOU BRING BACK FOR ME?

© ASHLEIGH BRILLIANT 1980.

POT-SHOTS NO. 1887.

Ashleigh Brilliant .com

FORGIVE MY LITTLE OUTBURSTS,

AND BE GLAD THEY'RE NOT BIGGER ONES.

© ASHLEIGH BRILLIANT 1980.

POT-SHOTS NO. 1852.

I'M HAPPIEST WITH THOSE WHO KNOW AND LOVE ME ~

THAT'S WHY I'VE NEVER BEEN VERY HAPPY.

Ashleigh Brilliant.com

POT-SHOTS NO. 1788.

WHAT I WANT
IS
TO BE POPULAR
WITHOUT
HAVING TO BE
NICE.

Ashleigh
Brilliant.com

Well,
if you don't like
my opinion
of you,

you can always

improve.

© BRILLIANT ENTERPRISES 1968

POT-SHOTS NO. 69

I'M ONLY
HURTING YOU
FOR MY
OWN GOOD

Ashleigh
Brilliant.COM

POT-SHOTS NO. 1848

Ashleigh
Brilliant
.COM

THIS WOULD BE
A BETTER
WORLD

IF
EVERYBODY
LOVED
ME MORE.

©ASHLEIGH BRILLIANT 1980.

POT-SHOTS NO. 77

Ashleigh
Brilliant.COM

I BEG YOU NOT TO LEAVE ME
BEFORE I ABANDON YOU.

© BRILLIANT ENTERPRISES 1968

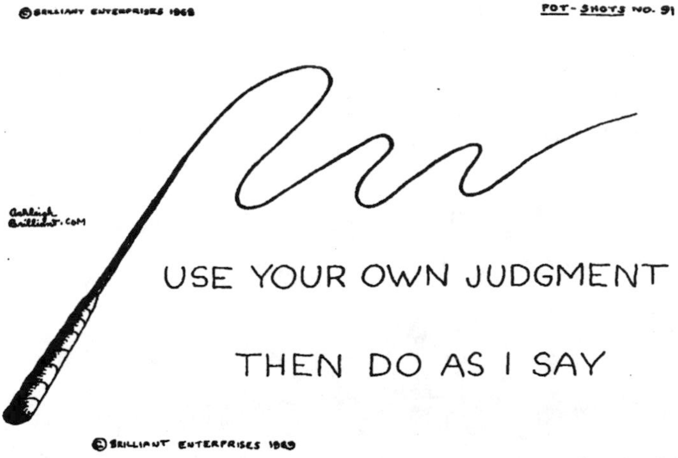

© BRILLIANT ENTERPRISES 1968

POT-SHOTS NO. 91

ashleigh
Brilliant.com

USE YOUR OWN JUDGMENT

THEN DO AS I SAY

© BRILLIANT ENTERPRISES 1969

IF YOU REALLY LOVED ME
YOU'D LET ME
KICK YOU MORE OFTEN.

POT-SHOTS NO. 1737.

ashleigh
Brilliant
.com

PLEASE
TRY TO BE
MORE FLEXIBLE,
SO THAT I CAN
MORE EASILY
TIE YOU IN A KNOT.

© ASHLEIGH BRILLIANT 1980.

POT- SHOTS NO. 442

WHATEVER THEY'RE SAYING ABOUT ME,

I DENY EVERYTHING!

AshleighBrilliant.com

POT-SHOTS NO. 1475.

MY LOVE MAY BE FALSE,

Ashleigh Brilliant.com

BUT MY HATRED IS ALWAYS GENUINE.

WHY
AM I ALWAYS
SO ALONE
IN
MY STRUGGLE
TO HAVE
MY OWN WAY?

POT-SHOTS NO. 1683.

Ashleigh
Brilliant.COM

© ASHLEIGH BRILLIANT 1980.

IF YOU MAKE
ONE OR TWO
RIDICULOUS
ASSUMPTIONS,

YOU'LL FIND
EVERYTHING
I SAY
OR DO
TOTALLY
JUSTIFIED.

Ashleigh
Brilliant

WE'LL
ALWAYS
STAY
ON
GOOD
TERMS,

POT-SHOTS NO. 1731.

Ashleigh
Brilliant.com

SO LONG
AS THEY'RE
MY TERMS.

©ASHLEIGH BRILLIANT 1980

©BRILLIANT ENTERPRISES 1968

POT-SHOTS NO. 140

HOW DARE YOU
GET ALONG
WITHOUT ME!

Ashleigh
Brilliant.com

©BRILLIANT ENTERPRISES 1968

POT-SHOTS NO. 46

WON'T YOU EVEN GIVE ME A CHANCE

TO RUIN YOUR LIFE?

Ashleigh
Brilliant.com

© ASHLEIGH BRILLIANT 1979.   POT-SHOTS NO. 1570.

WHY DO I HAVE SO MUCH TROUBLE FORCING PEOPLE TO LIKE ME?

Ashleigh
Brilliant.com

POT-SHOTS NO. 380

HOW CAN YOU CALL IT UNREASONABLE

Ashleigh
Brilliant.com

WHEN ALL I WANT IS MY OWN WAY?

© BRILLIANT ENTERPRISES 1972

© BRILLIANT ENTERPRISES 1972   POT-SHOTS NO. 327

I SEEM TO BE LOSING MY SENSE OF DIRECTION —

WHICH WAY IS STRAIGHT AHEAD?

Ashleigh
Brilliant
.com

POT-SHOTS NO. 1323.

AshleighBrilliant.com

DON'T BE
NERVOUS —

JUST REMEMBER:

ALL MISTAKES
WILL BE
SEVERELY PUNISHED.

POT-SHOTS NO. 1285.

I'M THINKING ABOUT
BECOMING
A BETTER PERSON —

DON'T I DESERVE
SOME CREDIT
FOR THAT?

AshleighBrilliant.com

POT-SHOTS NO. 1270.

ALL I WANT
IS TO BE TREATED
LIKE EVERYONE ELSE,

NO MATTER HOW
REVOLTINGLY DIFFERENT
I AM.

POT-SHOTS NO. 1779.

I'M ONLY
BEHAVING WELL
AT PRESENT

BECAUSE I HAVE
SO FEW
OPPORTUNITIES
TO BEHAVE BADLY.

POT- SHOTS NO. 506

I KNOW
WHO I REALLY AM

BUT I'M
KEEPING IT
A SECRET
FROM MYSELF.

Ashleigh
Brilliant.com

I DON'T LIKE TO BE
ACCUSED UNJUSTLY

OR EVEN
JUSTLY.

Ashleigh
Brilliant
.com

© ASHLEIGH BRILLIANT 1978   POT-SHOTS NO. 1488

WHICH OF
MY PROBLEMS
ARE YOU
WILLING TO TAKE
FULL RESPONSIBILITY FOR?

Ashleigh
Brilliant.com

© BRILLIANT ENTERPRISES 1974   POT-SHOTS NO. 463

I LIVE
IN A WORLD
OF MY OWN,

BUT VISITORS
ARE ALWAYS
WELCOME.

Ashleigh
Brilliant.com

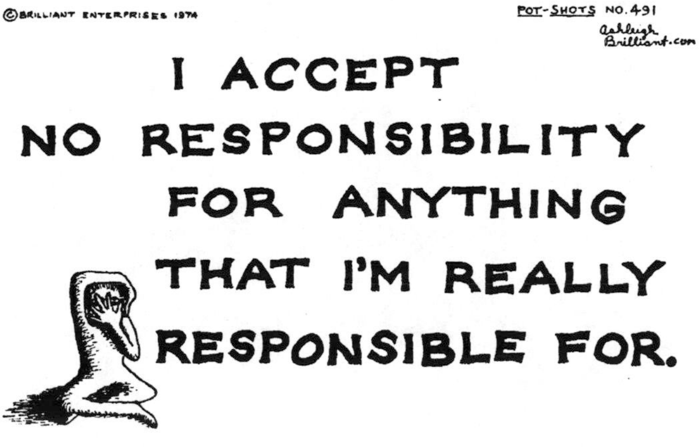

© BRILLIANT ENTERPRISES 1974   POT-SHOTS NO. 491

Ashleigh
Brilliant.com

I ACCEPT
NO RESPONSIBILITY
FOR ANYTHING
THAT I'M REALLY
RESPONSIBLE FOR.

POT-SHOTS NO. 1519.

**EVERY NOW AND THEN,
I DO
THE RIGHT
THING,**

**JUST TO
CONFUSE
YOU.**

©ASHLEIGH BRILLIANT 1979

POT-SHOTS NO. 405

To any
truly impartial person,
it would be
obvious that
I am always right.

Ashleigh
Brilliant.com
©BRILLIANT ENTERPRISES 1973

POT-SHOTS NO. 1464.

YOU CAN'T
JUST SUDDENLY
BE MY
FRIEND

Ashleigh
Brilliant
.com

YOU HAVE TO
GO THROUGH
A TRAINING PERIOD.

© ASHLEIGH BRILLIANT 1979.

POT-SHOTS NO. 1421.

Ashleigh
Brilliant
.com

SOME PEOPLE CAN FIND
ALL THE
PEACE OF MIND THEY NEED
IN A GOOD,
SATISFYING,
CONFLICT.

© ASHLEIGH BRILLIANT 1979.

POT-SHOTS NO. 1418.

WHAT GOOD IS FREEDOM,

IF IT DOESN'T
INCLUDE
THE FREEDOM
TO
TRAMPLE UPON
OTHER PEOPLE'S RIGHTS?

Ashleigh
Brilliant
.com

© ASHLEIGH BRILLIANT 1979.

POT-SHOTS NO. 1175.

WHAT'S THE GOOD
OF BEING
FORGIVEN,
IF I HAVE TO
PROMISE
NOT TO
DO IT AGAIN?

©BRILLIANT ENTERPRISES 1974.

POT-SHOTS NO. 671.

BREAK
ANY OTHER LAWS
YOU LIKE,

BUT DON'T BREAK MINE!

Ashleigh Brilliant.com

© BRILLIANT ENTERPRISES 1977

POT-SHOTS NO. 1155.

BEWARE!

I CAN DO
GREAT HARM
TO MYSELF,
AND BLAME IT
ON YOU.

Ashleigh Brilliant.com

© BRILLIANT ENTERPRISES 1977

POT-SHOTS NO. 1081.

PLEASE DON'T PUT A STRAIN
ON OUR FRIENDSHIP

Ashleigh
Brilliant
.com

BY
ASKING ME
TO DO SOMETHING
FOR YOU.

MY PROBLEM IS
TO PERSUADE YOU
THAT WHAT'S
TO MY ADVANTAGE
IS ALSO
TO YOURS.

Ashleigh
Brilliant
.com

©BRILLIANT ENTERPRISES 1977.

©BRILLIANT ENTERPRISES 1974

<u>POT-SHOTS</u> NO.525

IT ALWAYS HELPS PROVE
HOW RIGHT YOU ARE

IF YOU
WAVE YOUR ARMS
AND JUMP
AND SCREAM.

Ashleigh
Brilliant
.com

©BRILLIANT ENTERPRISES 1974.

<u>POT-SHOTS</u> NO. 605

Ashleigh
Brilliant.com

I resent
being treated

like the sort of person 
I really
am.

LOVE EXPRESSES ITSELF IN STRANGE WAYS --

Think of that

The next time

I attempt to destroy you.

Ashleigh Brilliant ·com

© BRILLIANT ENTERPRISES 1977.   POT-SHOTS NO. 1142.

ALL MY CRUEL ACTS
WERE ENTIRELY JUSTIFIED

BY THE
FACT THAT
I AM

Ashleigh
Brilliant.com

A VERY CRUEL PERSON.

© BRILLIANT ENTERPRISES 1974·   POT-SHOTS NO· 691

TAKE HEART!
Sooner or later,
You'll recover from
What I've done to you

Ashleigh Brilliant ·com

POT-SHOTS NO. 963.

THANK YOU
FOR LETTING ME
CRITICIZE YOU
SO UNFAIRLY:

IT MAKES ME
FEEL
SO
IMPORTANT.

©BRILLIANT ENTERPRISES 1976.

©BRILLIANT ENTERPRISES 1976.

POT-SHOTS NO. 946.

DON'T BE AFRAID
TO HURT MY FEELINGS:

ALL YOU RISK
IS MY
UNBOUNDED
RAGE.

I'm looking
for somebody
who wouldn't mind
having me
as an
intolerable burden.

Ashleigh Brilliant

Ashleigh
Brilliant.com

I DON'T
GUARANTEE
ANYTHING,

WHICH IS
LUCKY
FOR YOU,

SINCE MY
GUARANTEES

ARE
USUALLY
WORTHLESS.

I HOPE
YOU ENJOY
BEING USED
FOR MY OWN
SELFISH PURPOSES.

Ashleigh
Brilliant.com

POT-SHOTS NO. 924.

THE MORE
I HAVE YOU
UNDER MY
CONTROL,

THE EASIER
IT IS
TO
TRUST YOU.

Ashleigh
Brilliant.com

©BRILLIANT ENTERPRISES 1976.

©BRILLIANT ENTERPRISES 1977

POT-SHOTS NO. 1125.

TELL ME THE TRUTH!

EVEN IF YOU KNOW
I'LL MAKE YOU
SUFFER UNBEARABLY
FOR TELLING ME.

Ashleigh Brilliant.com

POT-SHOTS NO. 748.

Ashleigh
Brilliant.com

PLEASE LET ME KNOW

IF THERE'S ANY FURTHER TROUBLE

I CAN

GIVE YOU.

©BRILLIANT ENTERPRISES 1975.

POT-SHOTS NO. 1116.

HAVE I
RUINED
YOUR
LIFE,

Ashleigh
Brilliant.com

OR
WAS IT
RUINED
ALREADY?

© BRILLIANT ENTERPRISES 1977

POT-SHOTS NO. 1080.

HOW FAR
MUST I GO
AWAY FROM YOU

TO GET
YOUR ATTENTION?

© BRILLIANT ENTERPRISES 1977.

Ashleigh Brilliant.com

LET'S PUT THE
POT-SHOTS NO. 1083.
BLAME WHERE IT
BELONGS:

Ashleigh
Brilliant
.com

ON SOMEBODY ELSE.

© BRILLIANT ENTERPRISES 1977.

POT-SHOTS NO. 1002

You can't love me
as a hobby —

you've got to
consider it
a career.

© BRILLIANT ENTERPRISES 1977.

© BRILLIANT ENTERPRISES 1976.

POT-SHOTS NO. 929.

CONGRATULATIONS
ON YOUR
GREAT PERFORMANCE
AS A MEMBER
OF MY
AUDIENCE.

Ashleigh Brilliant.com

© BRILLIANT ENTERPRISES 1975.

POT-SHOTS NO. 843.

It's possible that
my whole purpose in life
is simply to serve as
a warning to others.

Ashleigh Brilliant.com

© ASHLEIGH BRILLIANT 1980.

POT-SHOTS NO. 1956.

I HAVE TO LIVE WITH MYSELF,

SO
I HAVE TO
TOLERATE
MANY
THINGS
I DISLIKE
ABOUT
ME.

POT-SHOTS
NO. 1993.

I MUST LEARN TO TAKE PLEASURE IN SIMPLE THINGS ~

SUCH AS
BEING
WORSHIPPED
BY HUGE
CROWDS.

© ASHLEIGH BRILLIANT 1980.

© ASHLEIGH BRILLIANT 1980.

POT-SHOTS
NO. 1963

THE TIME
TO START
WORRYING
IS WHEN
YOU BEGIN
TO BELIEVE
YOUR
OWN
LIES.

© ASHLEIGH BRILLIANT 1980

POT-SHOTS
NO 2010.

The trouble
with my life
is that
I keep getting
what
I deserve.

© ASHLEIGH BRILLIANT 1980.

POT-SHOTS NO. 1985.

I WAS GOING
FROM THE PAST
TO THE FUTURE,
BUT SOMEHOW
GOT PERMANENTLY
TRAPPED
IN THE PRESENT.

Ashleigh
Brilliant.com

POT-SHOTS NO. 2195.

SOMEBODY
INSIDE ME
DOESN'T
LIKE ME.

© ASHLEIGH BRILLIANT 1981.

Ashleigh
Brilliant
.com

POT-SHOTS
NO. 2298.

MANY
PEOPLE
DON'T REALIZE
MY IMPORTANCE
IMMEDIATELY,

AND
A
SURPRISING
NUMBER
NEVER
REALIZE IT
AT ALL.

Ashleigh
Brilliant
.com

© ASHLEIGH BRILLIANT 1981.

© ASHLEIGH BRILLIANT 1982.

PLEASE
COME BACK!
THE DOOR OF
YOUR OLD CAGE
IS ALWAYS OPEN.

Ashleigh
Brilliant .com

NOBODY
HAS EVER
LOVED ME

THE WAY
I REALLY
THINK

EVERYBODY
SHOULD
LOVE ME.

© ASHLEIGH BRILLIANT 1980.

POT-SHOTS
NO. 2040.
ashleigh
Brilliant
.com

MY
COMPUTER
MUST BE
BROKEN ~

WHENEVER
I ASK
A WRONG QUESTION,
IT GIVES
A WRONG ANSWER.

POT-SHOTS NO. 2338.

WHY AREN'T YOU MORE GRATEFUL

FOR THE VERY LITTLE I SO GRUDGINGLY GIVE?

Ashleigh Brilliant

© ASHLEIGH BRILLIANT 1981.

© ASHLEIGH BRILLIANT 1983.

POT-SHOTS NO. 2692.

I'M WORRIED BY THE POSSIBILITY THAT PEOPLE WHO KEEP REJECTING ME ARE NOT MAKING A BIG MISTAKE.

POT-SHOTS NO. 2696.
Ashleigh
Brilliant
.com

ALL
I WANT
IS A
LITTLE
THING
CALLED

TOTAL SATISFACTION.

©ASHLEIGH BRILLIANT 1983.

MY OBJECT IS
TO WIN
EVERYBODY'S
RESPECT,

POT-SHOTS NO. 2663.
Ashleigh
Brilliant
.com

AND
THEREBY PROVE
WHAT A BIG FOOL
EVERYBODY IS.

©ASHLEIGH BRILLIANT 1982.

©ASHLEIGH BRILLIANT 1983.

POT-SHOTS NO. 2705.
Ashleigh
Brilliant
.com

WHY HAVEN'T YOU
BEEN WAITING
MORE EAGERLY
TO HEAR FROM ME?

© ASHLEIGH BRILLIANT 1983.

POT-SHOTS NO. 2840.

SOMETIMES
THE ATTENTION
I GET
IS WORTH
THE PAIN
I INFLICT
ON MYSELF
TO GET IT.

Ashleigh
Brilliant.com

© ASHLEIGH BRILLIANT 1983.

POT-SHOTS NO. 2786.

DON'T YOU
WISH
YOU
MISSED ME
MORE?

Ashleigh Brilliant.com

© ASHLEIGH BRILLIANT 1983.

POT-SHOTS NO. 2905.

ONE FORM OF ATTRACTION
IS TO MAKE PEOPLE
WANT TO COME CLOSE ENOUGH
TO KILL YOU.

Ashleigh
Brilliant.com

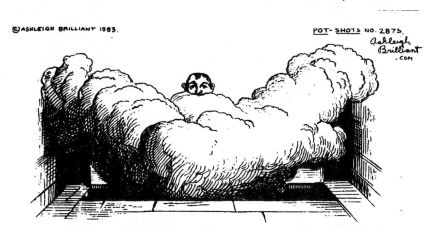

WHY SHOULD I LET YOU INTO MY PRIVATE HELL?

POT-SHOTS NO. 2968.

IF I WERE YOU, I WOULD BE VERY NICE TO ME.

POT-SHOTS NO. 3037.

CORRECT ME IF I'M WRONG,

AT YOUR OWN RISK.

©ASHLEIGH BRILLIANT 1983.

POT-SHOTS NO.2986.

IT'S
MY SAD DUTY
TO ASK YOU
TO BELIEVE
ANOTHER ONE
OF
MY LIES.

AshleighBrilliant.com

©ASHLEIGH BRILLIANT 1983

POT-SHOTS NO. 3094.

Ashleigh
Brilliant
.com

Most of us
are to some extent
insane,
but have learned
how to control
our insanity.

©ASHLEIGH BRILLIANT 1983.

POT-SHOTS NO. 3096.

If you
behave
yourself,

I'LL
CONTINUE
TO LET YOU
DO THINGS
FOR ME.

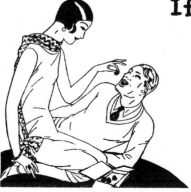

© ASHLEIGH BRILLIANT 1985

POT-SHOTS NO. 3174.

Ashleigh
Brilliant
.com

PLEASE DON'T JUDGE ME

BY WHAT I SAY

OR DO

OR THINK

OR REALLY AM.

POT-SHOTS NO. 3181

EVEN IF I'M SOMETIMES UNFAITHFUL,

YOU'LL
ALWAYS BE
THE PERSON
I WANT TO BE
UNFAITHFUL TO.

© ASHLEIGH BRILLIANT 1985.

Ashleigh Brilliant
.com

© ASHLEIGH BRILLIANT 1985.

POT-SHOTS NO. 3225

ALL I NEED FOR TOTAL CONTROL

Ashleigh
Brilliant.com

IS FOR
EVERYBODY ELSE
TO BE
TOTALLY
SUBMISSIVE.

POT-SHOTS NO. 3104. ©ASHLEIGH BRILLIANT 1983.

I KNOW
THERE IS
SOMETHING
TROUBLING
YOU ~

IS IT ME?

Ashleigh Brilliant.com

©ASHLEIGH BRILLIANT 1983.

POT-SHOTS NO. 3111.

Ashleigh
Brilliant
.com

HOW CAN YOU
POSSIBLY
CONSIDER
YOUR OWN
HAPPINESS
MORE
IMPORTANT
THAN MINE?

© ASHLEIGH BRILLIANT 1983.

POT-SHOTS NO. 3152

WHEN
DO YOU
WANT
YOUR NEXT
LESSON
IN
HOW TO
PLEASE
ME?

© ASHLEIGH BRILLIANT 1985.

POT-SHOTS NO. 3265.

Ashleigh
Brilliant
.COM

ONE OF THE THINGS
I MOST
ENJOY
RECEIVING

IS
OBEDIENCE.

© ASHLEIGH BRILLIANT 1985. Ashleigh Brilliant.com POT-SHOTS NO. 3393.

NOT
ENOUGH
PROGRESS
IS BEING
MADE

*by you
towards me.*

© ASHLEIGH BRILLIANT 1985. POT-SHOTS NO. 3285.

HOW WOULD YOU RATE ME,

ON A SCALE OF

WONDERFUL

TO

MARVELOUS?

Ashleigh Brilliant
.com

© ASHLEIGH BRILLIANT 1985. POT-SHOTS NO. 3522.

IF YOU MUST KEEP GROANING,

PLEASE
TRY
TO
DO IT
IN A RHYTHM
I CAN
DANCE
TO.

Ashleigh Brilliant.com

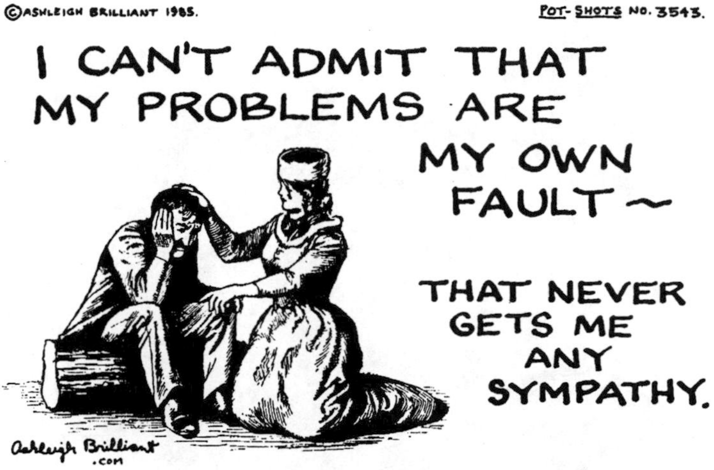

©ASHLEIGH BRILLIANT 1985.　　　　POT-SHOTS NO. 3543.

I CAN'T ADMIT THAT
MY PROBLEMS ARE
　　MY OWN
　　FAULT ~

THAT NEVER
GETS ME
ANY
SYMPATHY.

Ashleigh Brilliant
.com

©ASHLEIGH BRILLIANT 1985.　　POT-SHOTS NO. 3598.

Ashleigh
Brilliant
.com

WHAT MAKES
LIFE SO DIFFICULT
IS THAT
PEOPLE ARE ALWAYS
ON THEIR GUARD
AGAINST
PEOPLE LIKE ME.

©ASHLEIGH BRILLIANT 1985.　　　POT-SHOTS NO. 3563.

WHY DOES
NEARLY EVERYBODY
NEARLY ALWAYS
HAVE SOMETHING
MORE IMPORTANT
TO BE
CONCERNED ABOUT
THAN
MY
HAPPINESS?

© ASHLEIGH BRILLIANT 1985.

POT-SHOTS NO. 3304.

THERE'S NOTHING ON MY MIND

THAT COULDN'T BE EXPRESSED BY A LONG INSANE OUTBURST OF HYSTERICAL RAGE.

Ashleigh Brilliant .COM

© ASHLEIGH BRILLIANT 1985.

POT-SHOTS NO. 3307.

WHY SHOULD I ASK FOR HELP,

WHEN, IN A PERFECT WORLD, IT WOULD COME WITHOUT MY ASKING?

© ASHLEIGH BRILLIANT 1985

POT-SHOTS NO. 3314.

I ALWAYS WIN — YOU ALWAYS LOSE —

WHAT COULD BE FAIRER THAN THAT?

Ashleigh Brilliant .com

© ASHLEIGH BRILLIANT 1985.

POT-SHOTS NO. 3573.

WHY SHOULD I GIVE YOU REASONS FOR MY OBNOXIOUS BEHAVIOR,

WHEN THAT MIGHT HELP YOU ALTER IT?

Ashleigh Brilliant.com

POT-SHOTS No. 3855.

Can it be
that I have
the kind of
charm
best enjoyed

at a distance?

Ashleigh Brilliant .com

I'LL GLADLY
GIVE
FULL SUPPORT
TO ANY GROUP
WHOSE SOLE PURPOSE
IS
TO PROMOTE
MY PERSONAL INTERESTS.

POT-
SHOTS
NO. 3871.

What right
has anybody else
to remember
anything
about me
which I myself
have chosen
to forget?

© ASHLEIGH BRILLIANT 1987.   POT-SHOTS NO. 4080.

MY PARENTS INSIST
THE WORLD DID NOT
BEGIN WITH MY BIRTH,

BUT IT'S ALWAYS
POSSIBLE
THEY'RE
MISTAKEN.

Ashleigh
Brilliant.com

© ASHLEIGH BRILLIANT 1985.   POT-SHOTS NO. 3913.

Ashleigh
Brilliant.com

MY TIME
IS FAR TOO
VALUABLE

FOR ME
TO SPEND
ANY OF IT
TRYING TO
IMPROVE
MYSELF.

© ASHLEIGH
BRILLIANT
1987.   POT-SHOTS
NO. 4271.

WHY
ARE YOU SO
UN-COOPERATIVE,

WHENEVER
I HAVE YOU
UNDER
ATTACK?

POT-SHOTS NO. 3869.

MY ONLY HOPE
LIES IN
YOUR NEVER
FINDING OUT
HOW MUCH
I REALLY
NEED YOU.

Ashleigh Brilliant

POT-SHOTS NO. 3875.

HOW CAN
PEOPLE BE
SO UNAWARE
OF MY
CAREFULLY
CONCEALED
UNHAPPINESS?

© ASHLEIGH BRILLIANT 1987.

POT-SHOTS NO. 4006

WE CAN HAVE A WONDERFUL RELATIONSHIP,

AS LONG AS YOU STAY AWAY FROM CERTAIN VERY SENSITIVE AREAS.

) ASHLEIGH BRILLIANT 1988.

POT-SHOTS NO. 4423.

I'VE DISCOVERED MORE WAYS I'M RIGHT AND YOU'RE WRONG

~ AREN'T YOU ANXIOUS TO HEAR THEM?

Ashleigh Brilliant

POT-SHOTS NO. 4406.

Ashleigh Brilliant .COM

YES, I DO NEED YOU,

BUT IT'S ENTIRELY FOR YOUR OWN GOOD.

©ASHLEIGH BRILLIANT 1988.

©ASHLEIGH BRILLIANT 1988.

POT-SHOTS NO. 4414.

Ashleigh Brilliant .COM

Never stop seeking

new ways to please me~

but don't abandon any of the old ones.

POT-SHOTS NO. 4417   Ashleigh Brilliant .COM

ALL I ASK IS THAT YOU CONTINUE INDEFINITELY TO LET ME TAKE ADVANTAGE OF YOUR GOOD NATURE.

©ASHLEIGH BRILLIANT 1988.

© ASHLEIGH BRILLIANT 1988.   POT-SHOTS NO. 4466.

FORTUNATELY, THERE'S CONSIDERABLE DIFFERENCE

BETWEEN
WHAT
PEOPLE
THINK
OF ME

AND WHAT
THEY CAN
DO ABOUT IT.

Ashleigh
Brilliant
.com

© ASHLEIGH BRILLIANT 1988.   POT-SHOTS NO. 4602.

DESPITE WHAT MANY PEOPLE APPARENTLY BELIEVE,

THERE IS
NO SUCH THING
AS
A RIGHT
TO
ANNOY ME.

Ashleigh Brilliant .com

© ASHLEIGH BRILLIANT 1988.   POT-SHOTS NO. 4550.

Ashleigh
Brilliant
.com

WHY DOESN'T THE WORLD MAKE MORE OF AN EFFORT TO UNDERSTAND ME?

POT-SHOTS NO. 4430.

I'M NEVER TOO BUSY TO SAY NO!

©ASHLEIGH BRILLIANT 1988.

Ashleigh Brilliant .com

©ASHLEIGH BRILLIANT 1988.

POT-SHOTS NO. 4615.

DON'T HOLD YOUR BREATH UNTIL I IMPROVE ~

I DON'T WANT TO BE RESPONSIBLE FOR YOUR SUFFOCATION.

Ashleigh Brilliant

© ASHLEIGH BRILLIANT 1988

POT-SHOTS NO. 4641.

I DON'T MIND BEING USELESS,

SO LONG AS
MY USELESSNESS
IS FULLY RECOGNIZED
AND APPRECIATED.

Ashleigh
Brilliant
.com

POT-SHOTS NO. 4611. © ASHLEIGH BRILLIANT 1988.

HOW
CAN I
RESPECT
YOUR
JUDGMENT,

IF YOU TRUST
PEOPLE LIKE ME?

Ashleigh Brilliant .com

© ASHLEIGH BRILLIANT 1989.

POT-SHOTS NO. 4-915.

I WAS
SANE
ONCE,
AND
DIDN'T
LIKE IT.

Ashleigh Brilliant .com
SANTA BARBARA